FOR JO AND LIZA WITH MORE THAN APPRECIATION

TRICIA GUILD
A CERTAIN STYLE

TRICIA GUILD

A CERTAIN STYLE

For Sharon and Richard
very best regards
Tricia.

N.Y.C. 2011

COLOUR, PATTERN AND SPACE

AN INNOVATIVE APPROACH

PHOTOGRAPHY BY JAMES MERRELL

TEXT BY ELSPETH THOMPSON WITH TRICIA GUILD

QUADRILLE

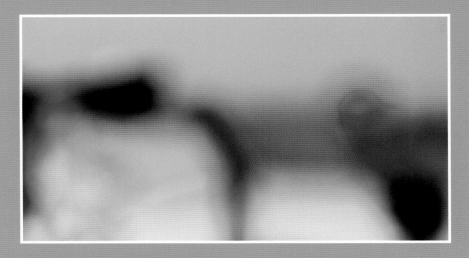
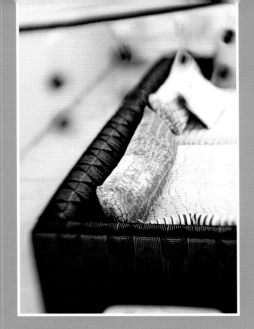

INFLUENCES AND INSPIRATIONS

I am often asked what influences my ideas when faced with the design of a new space. This book with its fourteen homes and fourteen very different personalities is my response to that question. Each project is unique and each has its own set of contrasting views – the views of the spaces, the views from the windows, the views of the owners, and my own view. Whether the space is grand or modest, traditional or contemporary, small or large, the challenge is how to approach each of these concepts whilst respecting the architecture but at the same time creating an atmosphere that is innovative, harmonious, filled with character and spirit. By using a combination of colour, pattern, texture and shape I hope to show how flexible these ingredients can be, how a certain style can be found, adapted and how a transformation can take place.

And transformation does take place... Often the same ingredients are used in different spaces and in quite different ways, demonstrating the adaptability of textile, colour and pattern and of contemporary, classic and vintage furniture. A modern interior attains individuality when an antique is added to the mix, and the reverse is also true – period rooms become dynamic and edgy with the addition of contemporary pieces. Fabrics trimmed and layered add warmth and informality; unlined banners can make a space more modern. Colour, a subject that I find totally fascinating, adds its own vocabulary with shades of the same palette, tones of neutrals, contrasts, accents, texture and much more, lending personality and vitality. Pattern can also be used to great effect – in one space in abundance, in another just one patterned cushion between panes of plain colour is all that is needed. Black and white features somewhere in most schemes, as I find its graphic quality vital. This intriguing alchemy creates spaces with character, soul and dynamic glamour.

With this book, I hope to stimulate ideas and creativity and show you how finding your own certain style can be a rewarding and enriching experience.

TRICIA GUILD

NTRIC

MODERN COUNTRY

BREATH OF NEW LIFE

It's a widely held dream to discover a sleeping beauty of a house quietly rotting away in the countryside and bring it back to life. This 18th-century stone farmhouse had been neglected for decades when its young owners found it and fell immediately under its spell. Looking past the peeling plaster and patchy roof tiles, they could see the romance and potential of the generous-sized rooms, wide oak floorboards and original panelled doors and fireplaces. After carrying out the necessary restoration works, there was not an enormous budget left for decorating, but the interiors have been transformed by an inspired mixture of pattern and colour, modern and vintage, classic and quirky touches. The result is a renovation project that goes way beyond restoring former glories to create a fresh and contemporary home within a period frame.

The simple grandeur of the surrounding countryside provided inspiration for allowing the natural scale of the interiors room to breathe, while building up an adventurous mix of colour, pattern and texture. The cool lime yellow of the entrance hall – an echo of the sunlight filtered through leaves outside – is carried into the drawing room beyond, with graphic black-and-white patterned wallpapers providing the backdrop for a mixture of new and old furnishings – curvy vintage sofas upholstered in a modern patchwork of stripes and flowers; contemporary chairs whose hard lines are softened by bright velvet cushions; flea market finds enlivened by a lick of white paint or a length of bobble trim. Each room has its own identity, but the whole house feels balanced and harmonious.

CONTROLLED COLOUR AND PATTERN

Pattern is key to the impression of accessible grandeur in these ground floor rooms – and limiting the colour palette, as here in the morning room, to black and white and just a few other key shades allows the adventurous layering of florals, stripes and damasks in a range of different textures to look rich yet harmonious and never overpowering. The patterns are often modern takes on classic etchings and damasks, but are used in an uncompromisingly contemporary way – note the mismatched curtains, the floral linen on the right lined with an inner length of smart black-and-white striped silk with a bobble trim that is echoed on lamps and cushions.

PALE SHADES, COMFORTABLE SPACES

Dining rooms can be forgotten spaces: seldom used and sometimes slightly stuffy as a result. Here, a lightness of touch has transformed the room into a pleasant venue for serving drinks, or simply curling up with a book. Just as the heavy wooden doors throughout the house have been painted neutral shades of white and pale grey, some pieces of dark period furniture – such as this table and its pair in the sitting room – have been given new life with a lick of white paint. Curves predominate, with a retro sofa, French wrought-iron vintage chairs, lamps and cushions upholstered in a lively mismatch of black-and-white patterns, the colours of which are continued into the sitting room and study beyond.

RICH COLOURS AND TEXTURES

In this house the principal patterns used are always of a similar scale, creating harmony and giving the rooms a familiar 'weight' or feel in spite of other changes. In the drawing room there is a subtle shift in colour, the soft yellow of the entrance hall and sitting room enlivened by warm pink and lilac. Rather than a graphic print, the walls here are a subtle flock damask in pale crocus colours that are picked up in the stripes and floral fabrics used for the furnishings. The furniture, on the other hand, is never of one single style: here the contemporary tweed sofas are joined by a classic painted console, vintage wrought-iron table, quirky lampshades and a marble Saarinen table.

MOVING UPSTAIRS

One of the pleasures of exploring an unfamiliar house, or walking through your own home, is the way the different spaces open into one another, creating pleasing transitions from room to room and floor to floor. In this house, the subtle unity created by the colour scheme and scale of pattern help contribute to this enjoyment, ensuring there are no jarring shocks, only pleasant surprises. Period houses often have long corridors, which can be wasted spaces, and rooms with interior doors creating vistas from room to room. This house is no exception, and great care has been taken to create a harmonious progression throughout the place. Moving upstairs, for instance, the little landing with its view out over the garden includes all of the colours to be found on both floors of the house, with soft powder blues and pinks mingling with the acid yellow and aqua. A table, some flowers, a seat to admire the view, all invite you to pause and appreciate this step on the journey. There are similar touches on the upper floor corridor, with different patterned curtains framing the views out, and papers and paints in complementary patterns and colours creating a series of settings through which the rooms and spaces beyond can be glimpsed. The eye is continually moving from the detail in the foreground – flowers, pictures, the patterns on fabric and paper – to the more distant space beyond, registering the subtlest progressions of colour, style and mood as it goes. Yellow turns to soft duck-egg blue, and the graphic flower pattern on the walls is juxtaposed with the soft, calm stripes of the silk curtains adding a tailored feeling.

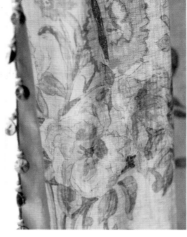

ROSES AND RIBBONS

On the first floor the mood is softer, the patterns less graphic and the palette more delicate than downstairs. Here in the master bedroom, this beautiful rose-and-ribbon print is the star of the show, setting the scene with its pale aqua ground enlivened with moss green (continuity from downstairs) and several shades of pink which are echoed throughout the room, right down to the details. Effort has been made to create a place that is not just about sleeping: note the comfortable chairs, upholstered in a luxurious textured velvet that's repeated on the bed, the mirrored coffee table and piles of cushions for reading in bed.

CALM SPACE

Leading off the master bedroom, the bathroom is painted a soft dove grey; the space is calm and neutral, with the same patterned curtains as in the bedroom, and a panel of the same wallpaper continuing beyond the doorway to ease the transition from one room to another.

SIMPLE TOUCHES

An antique roll top bath is perfect for the space, its exterior unpainted to show the patina of age. The wrought-iron chair and cabinet are painted white and the same soft dove grey as the walls, enhancing the sense of calm that pervades the room.

GLAMOROUS DETAILS

Luxurious little details make this a truly nurturing space. Note the chandelier, which catches the morning light, and the linen shower curtain, lined with plastic, that hangs from a circular chrome rail. Fresh flowers in the same soft colours as the curtains are arranged in small vases on a mirrored tray, with scented candles alongside – creating an air of romance right into the evening.

LILAC AND PALE AMETHYST

The upstairs sitting room has a luxurious boudoir feel. Soft colours in the same tonal range create a calm, harmonious atmosphere. Flock wallpaper and sumptuous silks in lilac and pale amethyst create an air of quiet comfort, while sheeny satins and gilded papers gleam softly in the afternoon light. Glass adds a lightness of touch – in the chandelier, the bead trim on the lampshade, the plain vases on the mirror-top table. The room is practical as well as beautiful, with the pair of day beds doubling up as extra spare beds when the house is full. Small mirror-topped tables are conveniently placed to take books, drinks and flowers.

GUEST ROOMS

One of the two tiny guest rooms could have become an ensuite bathroom, but it was decided to keep them as they are, capitalising on their small scale to create rooms that are like magical jewel boxes spilling over with delightful details.

STRIPES AND FLORALS

This bedroom can just fit in a double bed piled with cushions that bring together all the radiant colours in the room. The pink wall is a good foil for the floral curtains and the small pictures hung together which add to the intimate mood. Note how the silk stripe used at the windows is used on the back of the armchair.

VINTAGE CHARM

The other guest bedroom (overleaf) has a single bed, floral curtains and a patchwork of old foxed mirrors with a striped silk and beaded fringe (the silk stripe used in the other room). Both bedrooms retain their somewhat old-fashioned – but extremely useful – wash basins, made glamorous with fresh flowers, pretty perfume bottles and sweet-smelling soaps.

DYNA

AMIC

COASTAL RETREAT

COLOUR AND LIGHT

A dramatic setting calls for a bold yet simple design response. Perched on a slope above the sea, with its own adjoining pool, this modern house looks straight out across the bay to two colossal craggy islands – a commanding view in all weathers. Designed around this panorama, the building is so light it is almost transparent: a series of glass walls that can be opened right up to bring the view into the house and allow life to spill out around the poolside. When furnishing and decorating such a space, the aim is to find shapes, styles and colours that will neither detract from the setting, nor be overwhelmed by it. Here, a decision was taken to eschew pattern in favour of blocks of strong but soft plain colour that would be seen primarily against a backdrop of blue sky and sea.

The tone is set outside, where the wall that flanks the somewhat sombre front entrance is painted a chalky matt black: the lime bucket chair is the perfect contrast, announcing a love of simple graphic shapes and strong colour at the outset. The strong horizontals and verticals set up a tension that will be further explored inside and which help make the atmosphere so dynamic: the shallow stone benches on gravel; the sculptural stone totem at the end of the pool; the low leather chairs and linen-clad sofa against the tall slender metal columns.

Almost entirely open-plan, the ground floor is one fluid space, bound on one side by a long pink wall that shoots right out of the far end of the building to form a backdrop to the terrace. An homage to the Mexican architect, Luis Barragan – who would often paint one key wall a strong colour, often pink – it provides the perfect starting point for the colour scheme of the interior. It is refreshing to see pink looking so simple, unfussy and almost masculine in character.

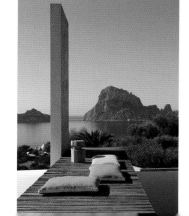

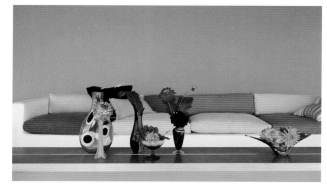

RELAXED SUMMER LIVING

Sliding glass doors, polished concrete floors and the long pink rear wall that continues out into the garden create a seamless indoor-outdoor space, perfect for relaxed summer living. Apart from the glorious cyclamen pink wall, the background materials are quietly neutral: pale resin floor, steel beams, white corrugated metal roof. Even the furniture itself is low-key: vintage Le Corbusier armchairs in soft white leather, a low steel table, a long sofa upholstered in white washed linen. Against this neutral backdrop a palette of pure Mediterranean colour used in bold blocks of one single shade sings out in great style.

POOLSIDE GLAMOUR

Relaxed indoor-outdoor living revolves around the pool, with comfortable cushions and loungers arranged at the water's edge. It's the perfect place for an al fresco lunch or early evening drink to watch the sun going down, and when larger crowds gather, more soft cushions – even a few with patterns – are brought into the mix, along with brightly coloured trays with glowing cordials and pretty scented flowers. Only a few metres from the house, the pool is sandwiched between the dramatic natural view on one side and the bright pink wall on the other. Often an uncompromising turquoise, the blue of swimming pools can be hard to integrate into some decorative schemes, particularly those using period patterns and florals. Here the pink of the wall, which actually has quite a bit of blue in it, is a shade strong enough to stand up to turquoise: and both colours partner well with the accents of orange, clear lime green and mauve that are used throughout. Sitting on the silvered wooden jetty, or placed along the low poolside loungers, the square coloured cushions enjoy their own moment of contrast with the blue of the pool, and even appear to increase its intensity.

INDOOR OUTDOOR LIVING

Floor, pool, sea, sky. Simple low shapes have exactly the right modern yet slightly retro feel, and serve to enhance, rather than distract from the view. The effect is akin to an abstract painting, with the larger blocks of colour being broken up by the bright pink, green and orange cushions that are placed on chairs and benches. Flowers in the same shades are placed singly, with contrasting sculptural leaves, in vintage coloured glass vases or floated in a wide-mouthed bowl. The eye takes in these small thoughtful details and the colour links between them, but is ultimately drawn back to the horizon.

GALLEY KITCHEN

In the little galley kitchen – connected to, yet hidden from the main space – the colour is provided by vibrant local produce. Empty and unadorned, this room would look almost clinical, but everything from the cups and saucers to towels and cleaning cloths has been chosen with colour in mind, while boxes of fruit and vegetables from the market bring it spontaneously to life.

FLOWERS AND FOOD

In a foreign country even the packaging of food and drink only adds to the glamour, enhancing the daily rituals of cooking and preparing food. Bougainvillea and hibiscus flowers pick up on the colours used for the furnishings; the pink cups echo the shade of the cyclamen pink wall.

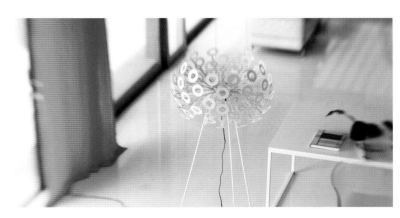

UPSTAIRS DOWNSTAIRS

Though the ground floor reads as one large room, careful grouping of furniture and lighting has created a series of spaces with different uses and atmospheres. At the far end is the seating area, with the enormous sofa positioned to take in the view. Nearer the kitchen, a white glass dining table is set perpendicular to the view, with modern swivel chairs with contrasting colour backs. Behind is that stunning pink wall, which stops well below the ceiling, allowing a strip of windows right along the top to bring in light, air and intriguing fragments of the surrounding landscape.

At the other end of the room, beyond the dining table, a spectacular wide, white staircase sweeps up to the first floor. At the top of the stairs, the pair of cool, airy bedrooms – similar in style but one in vibrant citrus shades and the other in relaxing aquamarine – provide peaceful private havens away from the sociable space below.

CITRUS BEDROOM

The master bedroom, situated at the top of the staircase, can be seen as one climbs up the stairs, and its colours have been chosen with dramatic impact in mind. A wall of clear bright yellow behind the bed provides a contrasting backdrop for other colours in the room, such as the lemongrass green and saffron curtains that can be pulled around the bed. Pencil drawn flowers on the palest yellow cushion add the only pattern in the room.

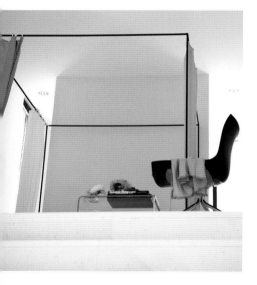

LIGHT AND AIR

The lightest and airiest of four-posters, constructed from fine extruded steel, brings height but not bulk to a small room, with the curtains taking panels of colour almost up to the ceiling. The other pieces of furniture – steel and glass tables and a sleek swivel chair – share this lightness of touch.

PALE AQUA SUITE

In this second bedroom and bathroom, paler cooler colours create a contrasting look and feel in a similar space. A pale aqua wall behind the bed is picked up by other shades of blue for the cushions and bed-coverings, while the curtain panels are plain white voile. The result is a beautifully calm, relaxing room.

SIMILAR ELEMENTS

For a pair of bedrooms, using similar elements but in contrasting colours and textures brings harmony and unity along with variety. As well as dressing the same bed in different coloured curtains, the same flower print in a different colourway is used for a cushion in this room, too. Such details rely on a calm uncluttered space for impact.

GLAMO

PARISIAN PIED-A-TERRE

ROMANTIC ELEGANCE

As a pied-à-terre in the heart of the city, nothing could be more glamorous than one huge grand room, with a tiny kitchen and romantic boudoir attached. The main space in this second-floor apartment possesses ballroom proportions, with wedding-cake white mouldings on walls and ceilings, a pale parquet floor and a trio of elegant French windows leading on to scrolling ironwork balconies. The already ornate shell dictated the look and feel of the scheme, which adds layer upon layer of rich pattern and luxurious texture to create a room that is extravagantly elegant and romantic. It's a case of 'more is more', and with its Marie-Antionette overtones, perfect for Paris. But it's practical, too: as the walls only needed the minimum of papering and the floor was too beautiful to cover up, the main effort and expense could be concentrated on dressing the wonderful windows, and covering an eclectic yet elegant collection of old and new furniture. Perfect for parties, or even a modern-day take on the artistic salon, the room is also a peaceful haven in which to relax and retreat from the pressures of urban life, curling up on the comfortable couch with a novel or contemplating the views down to the street far below.

The layering of pattern adds to the air of romantic luxury in the apartment, with damasks, printed and woven silks and florals framing windows, lining walls and piled high in cushions on chairs and sofas. Through all the rooms, however, the unifying and moderating effect of the tonal stripe can again be felt, with smart black-and-white stripes in particular used almost as punctuation marks: as decorative bows, on the backs of chairs and as trims on lamps and cushions – a reminder of the restraint and discipline that is present in true style, however opulent it first appears.

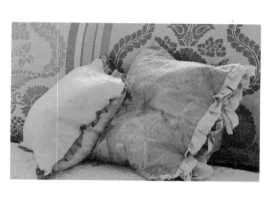

EXTRAVAGANT PATTERN

Working off the white and very pale grey of the paintwork, the palette for the huge drawing room was kept soft yet vivacious, with pale pinks, creams, greys and gold, enlivened by lots of fresh lime green and the odd splash of crimson. As the main feature of the room to be decorated, the three french windows have been lavished with layers of pattern: a lime-green woven silk damask, a flimsy striped white voile and a gorgeous floral print with gold embellishments that have been allowed to fall in extravagant folds on the floor. To counter them slightly, the blinds are in a somewhat more sober stripe in shades of green, white and ecru.

BOUDOIR STYLE

Concentrated pattern also appears in the tiny ante-room that leads in to the boudoir (see also previous page). Here, every surface is covered with flowers – printed, painted, embroidered and real, in every shade of pink and gold – to create an impossibly glamorous and intimate space that exudes romance. Sumptuously embroiderd silk curtains with charming velvet bobble trims, and billowing sheer voiles banded with ribbons of rose and gold softly filter the light to create an atmosphere of intimacy, privacy and serenity.

PEACEFUL DREAMS

The bedroom itself (left) is calmer – a predominantly white and pale-pinks scheme creates a peaceful room for sleeping. Vintage furniture looks right here: a pretty bed with a padded pink silk headboard and a curly metal café table next to it. Crisp white cotton sheets embroidered in pink, brown and gold are fresh yet romantic, as are the deep crimson roses at the bedside.

SOPHIS

TICATED

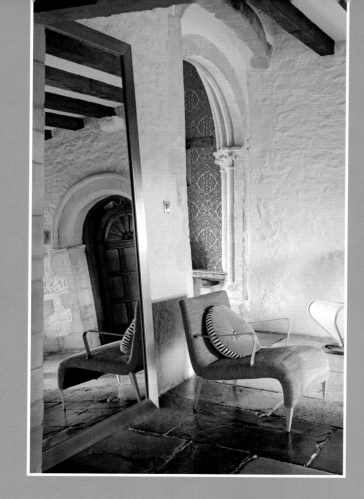

ENGLISH MANOR HOUSE

ANCIENT AND MODERN

This English manor house, with its eclectic mix of architectural styles, is the ultimate proof that the age and appearance of a building does not have to dictate the approach to its interior. Parts of the house are ancient: there are dark timber beams, flagstone floors, and stone arches that date back to Norman times. From the moment one sets foot across the threshold, the weight of history can be felt. Time was needed to get to know the house, work out how the demands of family life could be met within it, and to achieve a dynamic new look. Gradually, the right approach evolved: using bright colour and graphic pattern to breathe new life into the place while still respecting its history; to create a frame for modern family life within the old stone walls; to add another layer to the house's story rather than erasing its past.

With its stone arches, walls and floors and dark wood timbers, the challenge of the entrance hall opposite was to create a warm and dynamic atmosphere that sets the tone for the rest of the house. Painting the walls a pale dove grey helped to establish a fresh new feel and provide a backdrop for an exciting fusion of styles. The large mullioned windows demand a treatment that is visually bold as well as able to regulate light and temperature, so an unusual layering of colours and patterns has been built up: black-and-white striped silk, followed by bright turquoise, and then a crimson, orange-and-ochre-striped silk with embroidered flowers to add much-needed richness and warmth. Within this setting, classic contemporary chairs by Warren Platner and Tom Dixon seem just as at home as the grand piano, while a deep pile rug and banks of cushions add welcoming warmth and comfort.

JEWEL-BOX RICHES

Dark timber beams and panelled walls meant that this drawing room presented the ultimate challenge when trying to adapt the building for modern living. In some houses, one could paint the beams and walls, but here the original wood was preserved, so other means had to be found to bring in the light. Large expanses of white linen at the windows and a reflective white glass table certainly helped, but when it came to furnishings, a jewel-box effect was achieved with a mixture of luxurious embroidered silks and cut velvets in rich colours: crimson, orange, ochre and moss enlivened by plenty of black and white.

SUNNY STUDY
The panelled walls are perfect for a study, so a sunny corner of the room has been commandeered with a modern and masculine desk and chair. The dahlias on the top are the exact echo of the deep pink silk used for the curtains.

GLEAMING COLOUR
White curtains, sofa and table-top bring welcome light into the space, but the bright accents of crimson, moss and chartreuse have been chosen to gleam softly and intriguingly in the half-light. Flowers in these exact colours complete the scene.

SMART STRIPES
Black-and-white stripes on the ottoman and as backs and gussets for the cushions, with expanses of plain colour on larger pieces of furniture and rugs keep the atmosphere crisp and smart. By making a discreet reference to the geometry of the beams and panelling, the stripes help unify the room.

FLEXIBLE LIVING

This dining room has been decorated and arranged to create a flexible modern living space that doubles up as study and library. With only one window and an absence of dark panelling, the decision was taken to bring in as much light as possible, with walls in pale dove-grey, white linen at the windows, a white rug and white modern furniture. The two rectangular tables can be used separately as here, joined end to end to run the length of the room, or side to side to make a large central square. This is a simple way to create enormous flexibility in the way the room is used.

The far end of the room (overleaf) is a dynamic take on the traditional library: banks of thin metal shelves on a white panel displayed against a graphic wallpaper. To contain their random colours and sizes, the books are surrounded by plenty of white and the strong geometric pattern. Touches of pink in the padded footstool, flowers and vintage glass take splashes of colour through the room.

LUNCH IN THE GARDEN

Extensive gardens wrap right around the house, providing heart-stopping views from inside throughout the year, and a variety of places to sit in sun or shade when the weather is warm. Beside the enormous weeping willow, a simple metal frame is hung with banners of linen; this structure is used to define a separate space, creating an outdoor room with an intimate atmosphere. Here a table is often laid for lunch. A collection of antique garden chairs with bright linen cushions keeps the mood friendly and informal, with jugs of fresh flowers just gathered from the borders.

KITCHEN LIFE

In this large, bright room, where tall windows let the light flood in, gentle watery reflections enliven the space. Sunlight glances off softly shining surfaces: cool sea-green glass walls, a gleaming white corian table, granite and white marble work tops and the polished stone floor. Wide expanses of palest aquamarine give a relaxed, fresh background to a dynamic contemporary kitchen that is practical, invigorating and full of life.

KITCHEN VIEWS

The kitchen has an unexpected air of contemporary simplicity and a dynamic elegance. In the bay window, the black-and-white-veined marble used for the working surfaces has also been used to create a long low seat offering enchanting views of the garden, with a row of cushions lined up like counters in a game. Elsewhere, black granite defines the cooking area and the long refectory table is made from gleaming white corian. Against this backdrop, the bright Eiffel chairs, fresh flowers on the table and round washed-linen cushions on the window seats create splashes of vivid colour.

UPSTAIRS AND DOWN

Hallways, stairs and landings are great places to use strong colours and patterns where they can have a dramatic effect without having to compete with much else in the way of furnishings. They can also work like an overture, setting the scene and introducing the themes that will reoccur in subsequent rooms.

Patterned wallpapers can be used to superb effect on a double-height staircase. Here, for instance, boldly patterned wallpaper in strong colours helps dilute the impact of the dark and rather heavy wooden balustrading and the panelled doors and walls, and gives the entire space a more contemporary spin.

On the wall behind the stairs, a modern take on a floral damask design, in chocolate-brown flock on a duck-egg blue ground, adds a touch of glamour. A large, quite elaborate pattern, it is perfectly in scale with its surroundings, and the way the repeat falls creates diagonal lines that help lead the eye up to the floor above. The blue chimes in well with the blues and turquoise used in the room glimpsed through the doorway. It also echoes the rich gold and turquoise flock that has been used to turn the intimate entrance lobby into a tiny welcoming treasure box of a room. The brown of the flock is warmer than black, and sits well beside all the wood in the space: not only the balustraded staircase, but also the ancient timber beams of the fireplace and the natural rustic textures of the wood store. Tom Dixon's S-chairs and the chartreuse glass console add to the eclectic mix of the whole house.

SOFT COLOUR, GLAMOROUS TEXTURE

In the master bedroom and its next-door sitting room, a pale pink and off-white palette is sensual and luxurious rather than overly feminine. The tone is set by the bold damask pattern (top and overleaf) in pale pink on oyster-grey that is used to paper just one wall in each room, and it dictates not only the soft colour palette but also the glamorous textures of the materials: soft washed linen and flock silk on the chaise, pale cream leather and pink velvet for the sofa, a pair of Platner chairs with alchemilla seats, fine linen voile with a delicate stripe for the curtains at the four poster bed and windows. Matching square white rugs lighten and define the space in both the rooms – standing the bed on one has the effect of anchoring it on a calm white island as well as providing warmth and comfort underfoot. Behind the bed, doorways lead off to the dressing room on the left and bathroom and sitting room to the right.

DRESSING AND BATHING

Light streams into the bedroom through the large bay windows, bringing out the sheen on fabrics and papers, and bouncing off the polished wood floors. Framed by pink climbing roses, each bay window has a small table and chairs or modern daybed positioned to take in the beautiful garden views. Hidden behind the wall beyond the bed is a bathroom and generous dressing room which has rows of lacquered white shelves and drawers and a wall of mirrored cupboards. A door leads to the bathroom at the far end.

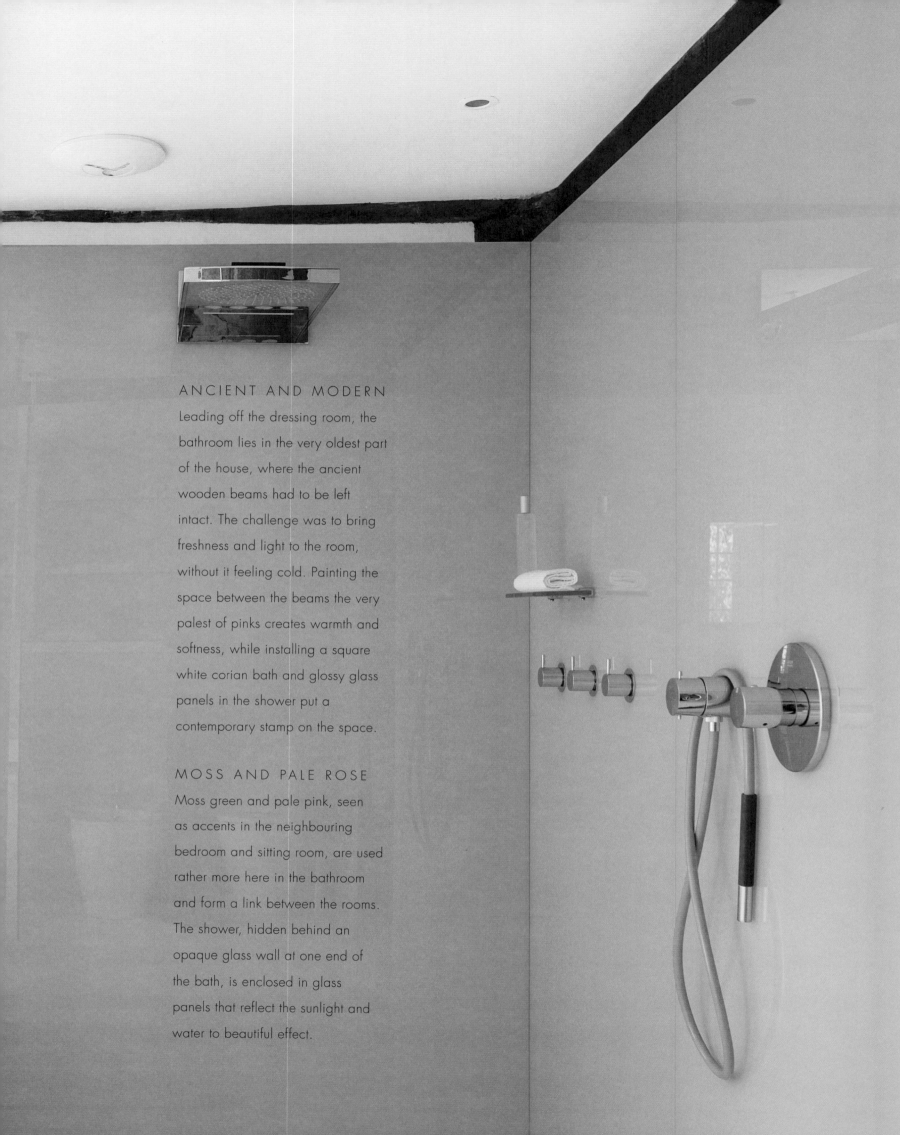

ANCIENT AND MODERN

Leading off the dressing room, the bathroom lies in the very oldest part of the house, where the ancient wooden beams had to be left intact. The challenge was to bring freshness and light to the room, without it feeling cold. Painting the space between the beams the very palest of pinks creates warmth and softness, while installing a square white corian bath and glossy glass panels in the shower put a contemporary stamp on the space.

MOSS AND PALE ROSE

Moss green and pale pink, seen as accents in the neighbouring bedroom and sitting room, are used rather more here in the bathroom and form a link between the rooms. The shower, hidden behind an opaque glass wall at one end of the bath, is enclosed in glass panels that reflect the sunlight and water to beautiful effect.

MODERN HISTORY

Right at the top of the house, under the eaves, a former attic has been converted into a gorgeous guest bedroom and bathroom. With its bare 'A'-frame beams and steeply sloped roof, this space could easily appear old-fashioned; but by painting floors and walls white and duck-egg blue, and installing sculptural state-of-the-art fittings, a fresh contemporary look has been achieved. Note how simple the curtains are: just a panel of voile with ties attached to a fine chrome rail.

Even in the bedroom, only modern furniture and fittings have been used. The juxtaposition with the strongly historical architecture creates a really exciting contrast: a unique pair of rooms with their own particular energy, and a heavenly hideaway for guests.

GUEST STUDY

With its views out on to the garden, this guest study-sitting room (left) is often filled with the dappled light of sunshine through green leaves.
To capitalise on this, and continue it even on dull or dark days, all the walls have been papered with this gorgeous leafy pattern in moss-green flock: summer sunshine on a roll.

TEENAGE KICKS

The bedroom shows how a good strong dose of colour and pattern can make a room with traditional wooden panelling young and vibrant. Two of the walls have been painted a zingy lime green that seems to bring the sunshine in, even on dull days. This green, together with a vivid turquoise blue, is used in the bed covers and cushions.

GRAPHIC TOUCHES

Graphic pattern is young and fashionable without being overwhelming. A grey and black rug, together with a Swan chair in white leather, add a Pop Art element, while one large storage unit helps keep possessions under control. In the bathroom (opposite) turquoise glass panels and lime-green fittings are energizing and vital

SPILLING INTO THE GARDEN

Wrapping around the house, and featuring mature trees and an old walled kitchen plot, the garden frames the house, providing beautiful views throughout the winter months, and a variety of sitting, eating and lounging spots all summer. Using rugs, parasols and giant cushions, another summer room appears.

SPIRIT OF PLACE

The garden was re-designed with Arne Maynard, who manages to fuse classic structure with a contemporary twist and a true sensitivity to the spirit of the place. Modern topiary, pleached pear trees, climbing roses on old walls and banks of fragrant lavender create a dream English country garden which still works as a setting for modern life.

VIEWS BACK

Looking back at the house through a haze of leaves and blossom, one gets a real sense of the history of this place, and of the lives of the present encumbents being but the latest chapter in a long and fascinating story.

PORARY

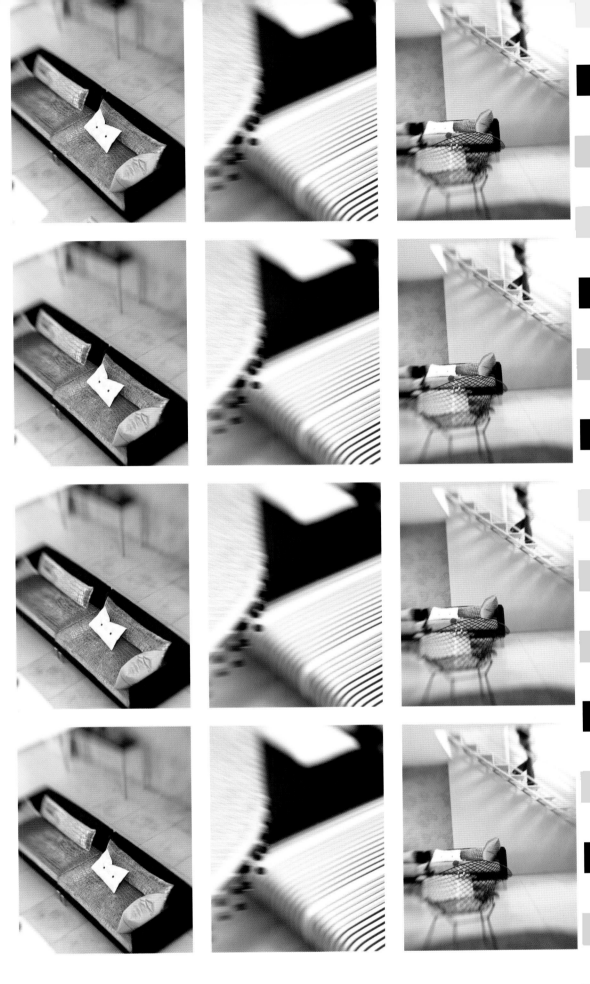

CITY PENTHOUSE

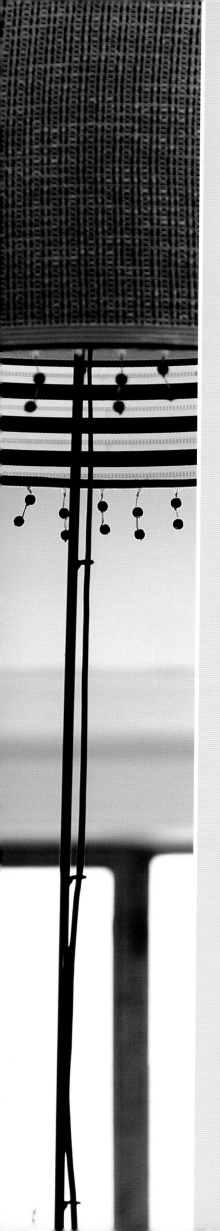

COOL SOPHISTICATION

A restrained palette, soft textures and masculine tailoring bring an air of subtle sophistication to this city penthouse. It's a meeting of opposites, with unexpected elements coming together to create a harmonious whole. What could have seemed a somewhat sparse, hard-edged interior with its floor-to-ceiling windows and vast expanses of pale stone floor, is softened by the use of beautiful textures such as cut velvet, grass-cloth, rafia and chenille. And while it is often deemed necessary to use strong colour in large white spaces, here the palette is disarmingly subtle, consisting of linen, grey and pale pink alongside black and white. Pink seems an unlikely choice in what is essentially a rather masculine scheme, but it works. Contributing warmth and softness rather than overt femininity, the palest shell pink is used here as a partner to black on the low modern tailored sofa, and as a foil for the sculptural glass staircase that climbs the wall behind. Used in this way, it works almost as another neutral.

The mix of pattern is also unexpected, and is inextricably linked to texture: a large-scale floral print on grass-cloth on one wall and a modern take on damask on the flock wallpaper opposite; an animal-skin-inspired design in cut velvet; a retro-style check in knobbly woven tweed; black and white geometry in rafia and chenille. Some interesting contrasts make for an extremely sensual experience as one moves about the space: from the polished concrete floor to the thick wool carpet; from the black metal Bertoia Diamond chair to the softest cushions in velvet, silk and washed linen. The result is a unique space that manages to be cool and sophisticated, and warmly welcoming at the same time.

OPEN-PLAN LIVING

One large open-plan space makes for flexible living, with different zones carved out by the placement of furniture. As the ceilings aren't high – the stairs lead up to a sleeping platform above – the shapes have been kept long and low, with this sleek modern sofa leading the way. Upholstered in an intriguing mix of textured black chenille and rafia and pale pink cut velvet with silk and linen cushions (see overleaf), it sets the tone for the rest of the scheme, combining a tailored style with luxurious comfort. Transparent furniture such as the wirework chrome dining chairs and glass-top table is great for contributing to the sense of space as their shapes don't block the view.

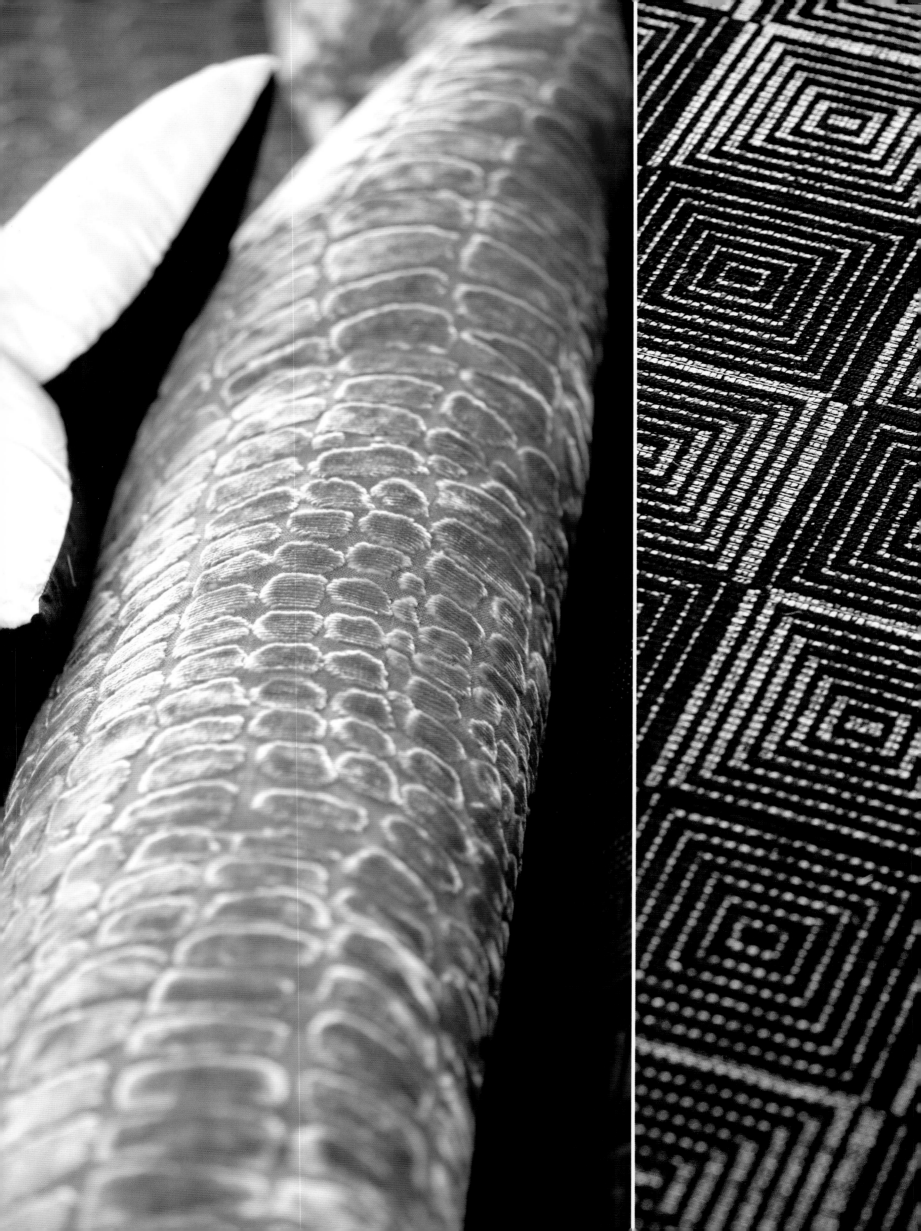

LIGHT AND TRANSPARENCY

The floating stairway, the large expanses of window and the light that floods through them give an airy open feel. At the windows, panels in a sheer black-and-white-striped linen can be moved across the panes to screen the light. At the far end of the room, a wall has been upholstered in a graphic black-and-white flock, which forms a dramatic contrast to all the pale colours.

Upstairs in the bedroom, a simpler monochrome flock paper calmly continues the theme. Bedlinen and accessories have been kept smart and minimal – a tailored yet luxurious feel, perfect for a guest bedroom where both men and women would feel at home.

BEAU

FRENCH CHATEAU

DELIGHT IN COLOUR

Strong, rich colour is not often used in period properties. It's easy to feel overawed by original features such as old panelling and plasterwork and think we should somehow 'respect' them by not using too much colour. And yet there is actually a long tradition of using very bright colour in such places: Georgian houses were often painted in strong yellows, reds, blues and greens, particularly in Ireland, as were Greek Revival houses in the southern states of America.

This small French country chateau is proof that bright, vivid, contrasting colour can breathe fresh life into a period building, working with rather than against the architecture to create a truly contemporary mix of old and new. In the hall and principal rooms there is a trio of colours: deep pink, bright turquoise and lime green are used in ways that pick up on the original charm of the building and accentuate it. In some rooms there is layer upon layer of pattern; in others mainly plains with the odd stripe – but there are always luxurious textures such as velvet, silk, satin and flock velvet everywhere. Crystal pendants hang from pretty lampshades and candelabra send glittering rainbows into every corner.

The scene is set in the entrance hall, where wedding-cake mouldings are accentuated by an elaborate flock damask wallpaper in deep crimson on gold that sends strong colour right up to the ceiling. The chairs are upholstered using the three key colours that will be continued elsewhere: a shimmering pink silk velvet for the button-back armchair and different silks and satins for the seats and backs of a pair of junkshop 'antique' chairs. Pretty beaded cushions in lime and turquoise complete the scene. Though contrasting shades, they are all the same tonal range in terms of intensity, which helps them sit together well.

RICH PATTERN AND COLOUR

This charming sitting room seems to break the rules, with layer upon layer of pattern and colour: pink silk damask, gold-printed flowers; turquoise velvet; lilac stripes. The effect is rich and luxurious, but it is quite controlled. There is only one printed pattern: the romantic overblown peony used for the strips of wall between the windows and as a curtain at one of them. The pink and turquoise curtains are the same silk damask in different colourways, also used to upholster the backs and sides of various velvet chairs. The soft mauve, black-and-white stripe used for a curtain is also used for all the blinds; and the cushions and flowers are all taken from the same palette.

GARDEN STYLE

Upstairs, with windows on to the garden, there is a great sense of the outdoors coming in. A flock leaf print on the walls accentuates this, as does the flower print at the window (the one from the sitting room, in a fresh colourway). Yellow and green work well with a dark floor: yellow washed velvet with a green damask back for the graceful chaise longue by Kirsten Horlim Holmquist, yellow vintage glassware and yellow-and-grey embroidered bed linen.

APPLE BLOSSOM

What could be more romantic than this pink and green boudoir on the first floor? There is a real sense of springtime with a palette the shades of apple blossom: pale and darker pink, white and fresh green leaves in the intimate sitting room, and a paler pink and olive green and grey in the bedroom itself. Lining green curtains in pink is a pretty touch, and lots of white in the floral fabric keeps the look fresh.

LUXURIOUS LAYERS

Layers of patterned fabrics on the antique bed: silk damask on the headboard, painterly floral linens, embroidered borders and graphic stripes. Piles of beaded cushions, garden flowers and pieces of vintage china keep the mood feminine, fresh and unpretentious.

125

QUIET LUXURY

In this airy study, the palette has been restricted to pale soft duck-egg blue, light grey and a pinkish oyster shade taken from the marble of the fireplace. This makes for a much quieter feel, but the mood is still luxurious thanks to the textures: cut velvet, washed velvet, silk damask and soft pink roses. Choosing the same pattern for the wallpaper and curtains has the effect of making the room seem bigger; the absence of a rug on the floor also contributes to the feeling of spaciousness. Again, the main colours are all of the same softer tonal range; and the chandelier has been hung very low to accentuate its beauty and draw attention to its effect on the light. Foxgloves and cow parsley strike just the right note of informal elegance.

VINTAGE

CHARM

TOWN HOUSE

SMALL HOUSE, BIG IDEAS

This typical urban town house is small in size but big on glamour. A few simple principles have enabled the owner to create an air of real luxury on a relatively small budget. First of all, the basics have been kept simple: painted floors, plain paintwork and unfussy curtains. The investment has been on a few luxuries that make a huge impact, including graphic patterned wallpapers, vintage pieces and beautiful woven silks and damasks that hang at windows. Enormous attention has been paid to the details, such as trimming lampshades and cushions with quality braids and tassels: small touches that contribute to a smart yet sumptuous overall impression.

The feeling of glamour is there from the moment the front door opens on to the entrance hall (previous pages). One long wall is entirely covered with a beautiful patterned wallpaper in turquoise and gold that sweeps up the stairs to the first floor. A gloriously frivolous design of flower garlands, swags and gold ribbons, it's a contemporary take on Rococo, and its impact is all the greater because the rest of the scheme is fresh and simple: white gloss paint on the floorboards with a wide strip of pale blue painted up the centre of the stairs like a carpet runner. The turquoise paper echoes and intensifies the paler blues of the paintwork, while the gold details pick up on the gilt relief on the vintage side table, the frame of the 1950s mirror and the gleam of the curly glass chandelier. The strong sense of colour, the mix of modern and vintage and the pretty selection of flowers and objects promises more good things to come, such as the gorgeous lime-green and pink sitting room opposite with its fresh young mix of modern graphic pattern, classic contemporary furniture and romantic vintage finds (see overleaf).

MODERN AND VINTAGE GLAMOUR

Higher ceilings give this sitting room a gracious airy feel that's accentuated by the use of pale colours. Petal pink and lime green is a fresh combination that works wonderfully in the bold flower-print curtains, the upholstery on the modern boxy sofa and the coverings of the pair of vintage chairs (see left – note how damask silk in contrasting colours is used for the seat and the back). Painted white floorboards keep things simple, and highlight the luxurious coverings on walls and windows and the presence of vintage mirrors and paintings. Black and white – here on lampshade, Swan chair, Saarinen table and cushions – is a strong presence throughout the house.

GRAPHIC CHARM

In this part of the house, while the rest of the furnishings are relatively simple the bold decision has been taken to use not one but two strong black-and-white patterns on the walls. A pretty large, graphic design is used confidently in a relatively small study. The dining room is hung with an even bolder, more architectural design: the effect is one of instant style and luxury, with just a hint of 1950s charm and eccentricity. Key to its success is that, though the patterns themselves are ornate, the restricted colour scheme – pure black and white with just the odd dash of bright pink – means the impact is smart and graphic rather than claustrophobic.

SLEEPING IN STYLE

The master bedroom is a tour de force — a lesson in how using careful amounts of glamorous pattern and texture can create an atmosphere of modern, uncluttered luxury. The pattern on the blinds and wallpaper panel behind the bed is the same as that used in the dining room, but this time in gold — which works well with the mixture of old and new furniture. Gleaming gold fabrics dress both the modern four poster bed and the antique Louis XV sofa — here the seat is in cream cut velvet. The sofa's gilded frame picks up on the golden theme, as do the pretty gilt and painted antique bedside table, and the grand large-scale floor mirror.

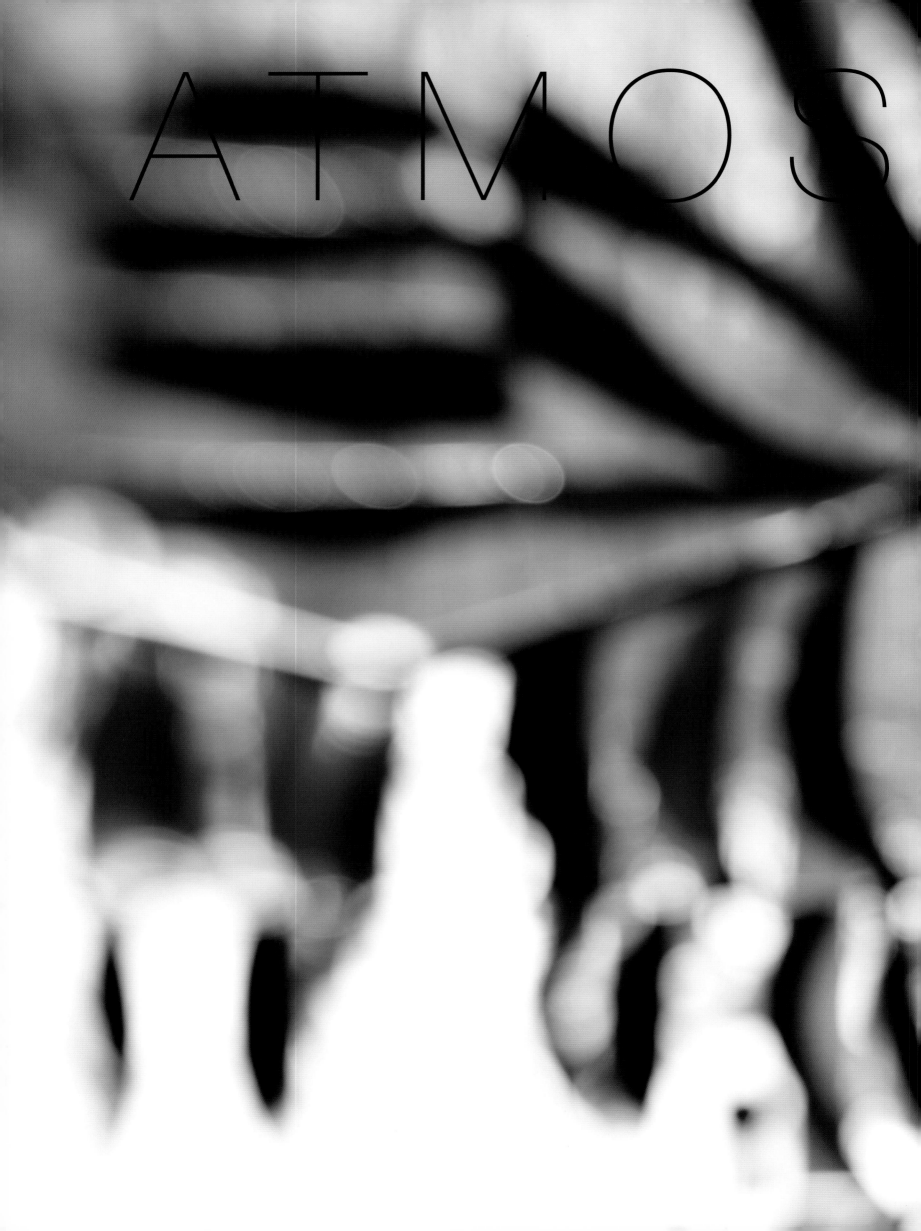

PHERIC

RETRO MODERN

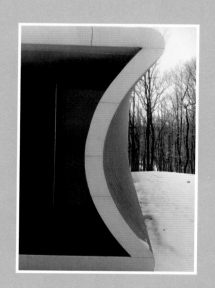

ART HOUSE

How do you decorate a house whose every aspect, from the entire construction and design to the detailing on floors and walls, makes it a contemporary work of art in itself? With its curtain glass wall and trio of tall white towers, this recently built weekend house in upstate New York looms majestically out of the hills like a cross between a 1950s space ship and a streamlined submarine. Inside, an innovative use of hard materials such as glass, concrete, plywood, coloured acrylic and steel work with the wrap-around wall of windows to create a spectacular open-plan space, flooded with ever-changing light. Cherry-wood pannelled dividing walls and a grey polished concrete floor create a stunningly simple backdrop for the owner's eclectic mix of modern furniture and artworks.

Faced with such a unique and individual space, the task was to find a way to enhance its wonderful features and contents without appearing to impose. In the end, minimal amounts of carefully chosen fabric enhanced the mood: graphic patterns that take their cue from the house itself (the radius curves where the beams on the extraordinary wall of windows meet; the shadows thrown by the Calder-esque metal screen at the front door), and in colours suggested by the owner's treasured collection of mid-century and modern ceramics — predominantly black, white, grey, yellow and orange. A vivid curtain in mimosa linen at the window; a few cushions made up for specific chairs; bold checked silk on beds and the glow of gold satin picking up the end-of-day sunshine — these might seem like small details, but their combined effect has a huge impact, bringing a vital layer of warmth and personality to the interior without compromising its individual style.

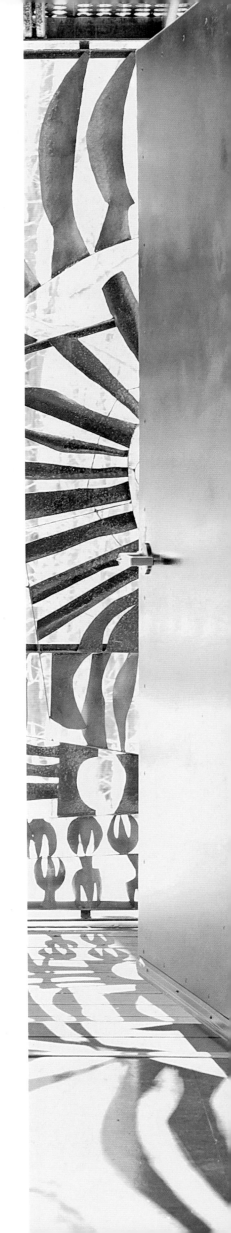

LIGHT MAGIC

A dramatic wall of glass windows runs down one side of the essentially open-plan living space, with cherry-wood pannelled walls dividing the sleeping areas from the main living space. There was some colour here in the collection of Guido Gambone ceramics, the classic cabinet, and in acrylic at the windows; however, the room now benefits from a careful injection of just a little more richness, pattern and lustre in the form of well-chosen fabrics such as the simple banner – in an acid yellow that works off the existing acrylic panels, furniture and ceramics – and touches of deep magenta.

KEEP IT SIMPLE

The house has its own built-in artworks, such as the bank of coloured windows and graphic metal screen, both of which work with the light throughout the day to create ever-changing effects. As the low winter sun shines deep in to the room in the afternoon, quite magical light effects are created.

Add ceramic treasures and classic pieces of modern furniture to this mix and it is no wonder that extra adornments are therefore kept to an absolute minimum. Just a retro-inspired design that picks up on the curved corners of the window panes, some smart graphic stripes in strong masculine shades and a little gold lustre to add depth and sheen.

COLOUR AND MOVEMENT

A vivid mimosa linen curtain breaks up
the enormous expanse of glass – and
can be moved along as a screen or
backdrop wherever required, filtering
the sunlight and adding new nuances
of poetry and romance. Flowers are
also important in bringing life and
movement to the interior, and the
tawny orange shades of the orchids
used here work well with the colours
of the furniture such as this Charles
Eames cabinet, a real collector's item.

ORGANIC COLOUR AND TEXTURAL CONTRASTS

The graphic shapes of the window panes, with their distinctive curved crossbars, make a striking backdrop to the kitchen, particularly with heavy snow outside. With the concrete floor, wooden cupboard fronts and lots of steel and dark stone, the only colour comes from the objects that have been brought into the space: the striped ceramic vase, the sprays of tiny orchids and acid yellow leaves, stray citrus fruit and the richly coloured stems of rainbow chard. Again, textural contrasts add another layer of interest, with the curious mouldings on the chair in the foreground and even the warm coats on the coat stand contributing to the mix. Note how art and nature provide the joyously unpredictable curves in amongst all of the straight lines.

NATURAL MATERIALS

Here in the dining area, again, small touches of colour inspired by the modern ceramics bring cheer and comfort. There is a lot of wood in this house, and bright fabrics and flowers define the beautiful table and benches that could easily get lost against the cherry-wood backdrop. Very thin padded cushions in acid yellow, neutral stripes and a beautiful dark purple make the benches more comfortable and inviting. Contrasting textures have been used, with matt cotton velvet alongside knobbly chenille and raffia, creating tactile interest. Keeping added colour and pattern to a minimum not only intensifies their impact, it also allows the natural light effects to take centre stage. As the light changes throughout the day, ever-shifting shadows create their own patterns across the concrete floor, enhancing its subtle sheen, while lozenges of pure gold are thrown onto walls and ceilings.

ABSTRACT LINES

Just off the main bedroom this bathroom, which is dominated by the intriguing curved wall seen in the exterior photographs on former pages, has a shower curtain made from the same acid mimosa linen used at the windows. The bold yet simple shapes of wall, granite basin and shower opening work off one another like the components in an abstract painting.

GRAPHIC PATTERN

In the bedrooms low sleeping platforms create an almost Japanese feel. Here and on previous pages, a strong black-and-yellow silk woven check and stripe again pick up on the colours used elsewhere in the house, and echo the graphic shapes of the Calder-esque metal screen outside the front door.

159

CHANGING COLOURS

The second bedroom is almost a mirror-image of the first, though using different patterns and colours, with two shades of magenta woven into the check, along with a subtle moss green. The retro-inspired square design, smaller black-and-white check and simple silk stripes are again echoing their use elsewhere – their repetition providing rhythm and helping to bind the various interconnecting spaces together. They suggest, also, how relatively easy it is to create different moods simply by changing the colour scheme and patterns used. In this house, as the amounts of fabric used are so small, it would be relatively easy to create a completely new look and feel by using different ones. Working with the seasons is one possibility, ringing the changes with lots of white linen in summer and warmer colours, textures and patterns for the winter months.

TRANQ

UILLITY

REGENCY COUNTRY

165

ENGLISH ECCENTRIC

Alongside the traditional 'English style' of chintz and pink rosebuds is a strong strain of 'English Eccentric' – the Brighton Pavilion, Chinoiserie and crumbling follies, the arty insouciance of the Bloomsbury set at Charleston House. It is this idiosyncratic charm – working with classic themes and patterns but giving them an offbeat twist – that has been captured in this delightful Regency house in the depths of the English countryside. Dating from the early 1800s, the architecture has the classic features and proportions of the period: graceful arched doorways, big bay windows and generous square rooms. It also has that lightness of touch that is synonymous with Regency – a delicacy in the fineness of the glazing bars between the window panes, a sprightly elegance in the curlicue scrolls of the ironwork supporting balconies and canopies. It is precisely this spirit that allowed and inspired the interiors on the pages that follow.

You'll find a bold use of colour and pattern – shades of Brighton Pavilion in the use of turquoise, canary yellow and orange, and a nod to Chinoiserie in the geometric patterns. There are flower prints, but with a contemporary spin: painterly roses in plain black and white, or huge embroidered carnations in deep crimson or chartreuse, accompanied by wayward chandeliers or lamps with mismatched shades. The irreverence of Bloomsbury artists can be found in the mix of patterns and objects: big bay windows have asymmetrical curtains; armchairs are upholstered in three patterned fabrics; ancestral portraits rub shoulders with designer chairs and shag-pile rugs. Underpinning the eccentricity is a discipline that makes it all work – a sense of order in the repetition of patterns, themes and colours; a subtle harmony of shapes and silhouettes that draws it all together.

GRAPHIC PRINTS, BOLD COLOUR

Shown here and on the previous pages is a classic English drawing room with a twist – or three. The components are all there – chintzy flower prints, comfortable furniture, standard lamps and chandeliers – but all just a little off-centre. Graphic rather than conventionally pretty, the flower print is in a bold monotone – black-and-white on the walls and with a bright turquoise ground for the curtains, which are hung asymmetrically and interspersed with black-and-white stripes and textured weaves. The furniture is beautifully tailored – a mix of contemporary sofas and stools with a pair of antique armchairs wearing smart but eccentric suits of damasks and black-and-white stripes. The tables are either vintage or state-of-the-art modern. The light fittings accentuate the quirkiness: beautifully made and decorated, but strung at odd heights or all with different fabrics and braids.

QUIET ROOMS

Using familiar patterns and colours makes for a smooth and stylish transition from room to room. This small sitting room and the little library off it have been decorated using a fusion of the blues and yellows elsewhere: the small blue geometric design in the main room is related to the larger print glimpsed through the far door, with the lovely turquoise flower print first seen in the sitting room on one wall of the library.

Limiting the shades of the patterns and stripes brings a sense of harmony to this suite of small rooms, making them ideal for reading or quiet conversation. Self-striped voile at the French windows filters the sunlight – two blue curtains and one yellow, while linen with stripes in a variety of widths and shades adds comfort on sofas and chairs. Note the continued unifying recurrence of the geometric patterns on cushions, lamps and rugs.

SOARING GEOMETRY

The geometric print on the walls is key to the unique mood created in the garden room, with its soaring ceilings and tall windows giving on to the conservatory. The pattern works well with the light in the room, and strikes a rather more masculine note than the rooms previously encountered, as does the colour palette of chartreuse, ecru, black and white. Like the flower print in the drawing room, this and related patterns recur throughout the house – sometimes in different colours, and often in unobtrusive touches, on lamps and cushions and so on, but enough to become one of the themes that draws the individual elements of this eccentric house together.

TEA IN THE CONSERVATORY

Opening out from the garden room is this spectacular curving conservatory. Many larger Regency houses had splendid conservatories, built not only to be decorative, but for growing tender plants and even exotic fruit for the household. They also made pleasant places to sit and stroll in winter – and even now, with missing panes and an air of genteel decay, fresh cushions in softly coloured shades of moss, pebble and primrose echo the luxuriant green leafiness that surrounds this pretty table and chairs, creating the perfect spot for afternoon tea in the welcome warmth of spring sunshine.

MIX OF STYLES

Wirework garden furniture is perfect, as it echoes the elaborate designs on the arches that frame the door. Much more interesting than a matching set of table and chairs – and so in keeping with the spirit of the house – is this mixture of old and new pieces. They work together as they are all wirework of one sort or another and painted white.

THE
MARCHESA
CASATI

LILLIAN BASSMAN WOMEN

FRESHNESS AND CONTINUITY

Particularly in a larger house such as this, using the same print in a different colourway in another room can create a fresh new look and feel, while also providing continuity. For the dining room, the flower print from the drawing room is used in acid yellow, which brings an air of sunshine to this rather dark room. Using the black-and-white version for one of the curtains — and the repetition of the black-and-white stripe and little lamps are also echoes from elsewhere — they set up a chain of association in the mind which is reassuring, like recurring themes in music. Lots of white helps to lift the effect of the dark wooden floor: a large white rug to anchor the elegant Tense table and chairs, and plenty of pale colours in the furnishings.

WARM COLOUR, SUBTLE PATTERN

A palette of crocus, pink and grey gives the master bedroom a fresh, feminine feeling; yet again the patterns are harmoniously linked to other rooms in the house. The subtle geometric print on the walls and the flamboyant embroidered flowers at the windows (overleaf) are actually the same as those used in the library and garden room downstairs, but the warmer colours make them appear new. The colours of the fabric were key when adding furniture and other details: matching the grey of the leaves in the painted table and textured velvet chaise, and the deep pink in the other chaise and the glass lampshade. The walls are painted dove grey below the dado and, above, papered in a small geometric design in pale cream and blossom. These small-scale patterns and textures read as plain from a distance, making a restful foil for the larger flower motif on curtains and cushions.

GRAPHIC PRINT

The Chinoiserie influence of Brighton Pavilion breaks out in this delightful guest suite, with its colourful mix of geometric pattern, smart black and white and rich crimson, orange and yellow fabrics. Once more, the injection of bright colour gives a fresh new feel, but look closely and the geometric patterns, smart stripes and florals have been used elsewhere in different colourways. Binding it all together, keeping it fresh rather than fussy, is lots of black and white: both in the strong graphic print on the walls, and in the plethora of quirky details. With its tailored stripes and perky pom-pom trims, this room is the interior design version of the style-conscious Regency dandy.

REFLE

CTIONS

LAKESIDE PAVILION

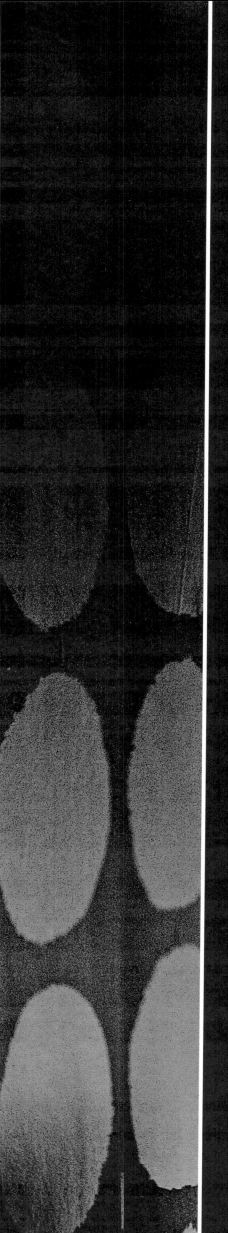

GRAPHIC PATTERN

This is modern architecture at its best – a simple glass-walled pavilion that seems to float on the still surface of a large lake. With serene views of the surrounding landscape as the backdrop, the challenge is to create distinctive interiors that enhance rather than distract from their setting. As the views are tranquil rather than dramatic, dominated by green hedges, lawns and trees, an excess of colour would be jarring. So the palette is predominantly black and white in the main living space, with accents of deep pink and moss green that are taken up again for the dining area and in the bedroom and study in the adjoining wing.

Cutting back on colour means one can still be adventurous with pattern. With their Op Art connotations, minimalist geometric prints are perfect for this style of architecture, and a variety of graphic prints has been used to define the main spaces. Just inside the front door, black-on-black circles are used to paper a section of wall and provide a foil for a black-and-white upholstered chair (opposite) – a dramatic entrance that leads seamlessly into the main black-and-white sitting room overleaf.

Repeating patterns in different colourways creates a reassuring rhythm as one progresses from space to space and room to room. At the far end of the black-and-white living space, a wall papered in a bright pink geometric print defines the dining area, while in the bedroom wing, the same pattern occurs in calming moss green, as do the Op Art diamond motifs. In the dining room, the print is repeated in contrasting colours in the trio of low stools that can be fitted together like a jigsaw, and – a clever touch – in the interior of lampshades. In the quieter bedroom and study there are no contrasts, only calm.

ARTISTIC INSPIRATION

In the main open-plan room the diamond pattern on the main wall and on a low moveable wall behind the sofa is almost Op Art, with a nod to Bridget Riley. A broad black-and-white stripe is used for blinds at the windows, and to cover a low stool, lamps and cushions. To break up all those straight lines, the outline of large flowers embroidered in black on white silk is used for a further blind, and striped with black on a lampshade. Pattern is used lightly, with expanses of white and neutral in the rugs and patterned velvet sofa. Colour at this end of the room is sparing: a vibrant pink on a Bertoia chair, a cushion and another sofa, echoing the wall at the far end (overleaf).

A MOVEABLE FEAST

Defined by the graphic pink print as backdrop, the dining area at one end of the living room is, quite literally, moveable. A shiny lacquered wood table on wheels can be pushed around, extended by adding another table, or double-up as a desk when not being used. Against the coloured backdrop, a trio of wittily trimmed lampshades are soberly striped with glimpses of vibrant colour on the inside.

QUIET SPACES

For bedrooms and studies, a cooler, quieter ambience is appropriate, and one way to achieve this is through a restricted palette. In this bedroom and adjoining study in a wing on the far side of the house there are no bright colour contrasts – just black, white and a soft moss green that merges with the surrounding landscape. The graphic wallpaper on one wall gives continuity and subtle interest.

E L E G

MODERN MANOIR

PATTERN AND TONE

Sometimes it is interesting to build a colour scheme gradually, starting from a base of neutrals and adding more depth and richness room by room. In this 18th-century French manoir, the entrance hall already seemed dramatic enough without a huge amount of colour or pattern to detract from the sweeping stone and wrought-iron staircase. So, using the existing colours of stone and iron as a starting point, a neutral palette of black, brown, cream, grey and white was built up. And though pattern is present – in the scrolling flower design on the staircase wall and the bold two-tone rug by the sofa, it is almost monotone – proof that even flower patterns can be sober and slightly masculine in feel. Moving into the next room, a small study with panelling to dado height, the existing paintwork was a typically French shade of grey; and to this neutral base have been added the dark charcoal grey used in the hall, a chartreuse yellow and pale mauve. Retro in feel, the flower print on the wall is given an up-to-date edge by this unusual colour scheme, and the mix of styles is highlighted by the clever use of the geometric design in the yellow rug and wallpaper that flanks the doors leading into this room. Mauve and yellow are a fresh and unusual combination with grey, but it is still a restrained and quiet colour scheme, perfect for a study.

Then, rather like an orchestra adding instruments as a piece of music gathers momentum, the palette is further enriched as we enter the large drawing room. Here, chocolate brown and crimson add still more layers in a crescendo of colour. Though all the rooms are very different, there is still a sense of progression, of consistency, a common thread that weaves its way through them all. And it is this creative coherence that makes good design work.

ILLUMINATED COLOURS

This drawing room is an exercise in how using dark colours with the right accents can bring real richness, drama and style. The addition of dark chocolate brown and cranberry to the broadly neutral palette used in previous rooms brings a delicious impression of luxury. It is easier to use dark colours on the walls when there is a dark floor to give weight to the scheme – and here the wooden parquet has been embellished with a large patterned rug with a chocolate ground that sets the tone for the whole room. On the walls, the brown background puts a slightly more formal, almost masculine spin on the pattern of crimson and white roses; the same print is used for just one of the curtains, while a broad silk stripe for the blinds and other curtains picks up the pink of the petals and the chartreuse of the leaves. See how the sunlight shining through them illuminates the colours like stained glass. All the other accents in the room – on upholstery, cushions, flowers, lampshades and so on – explore that same rich palette.

FIFTIES GLAMOUR

Upstairs, in an airy black-and-white sitting room with adjoining bedroom, neutral tones return, with a twist. An unexpected mixture of styles gives a touch of 1950s glamour with quirky modern lamps and retro furniture in smart striped felt, against a traditional trellis-and-flowers print on the walls. The monotone palette makes it contemporary, and the perfect foil to the bold graphic shapes and stripes.

BLACK-AND-WHITE CONTINUITY

The mix of styles in black and white in the sitting room is continued into the smaller, more intimate bedroom next door, with the same striped silk at the window, crisp black-and-white embroidered bed linen and a clever choice of two fabrics to upholster the scrolling vintage ironwork chair. Again, the black silk trim on lamps is a smart, playful touch.

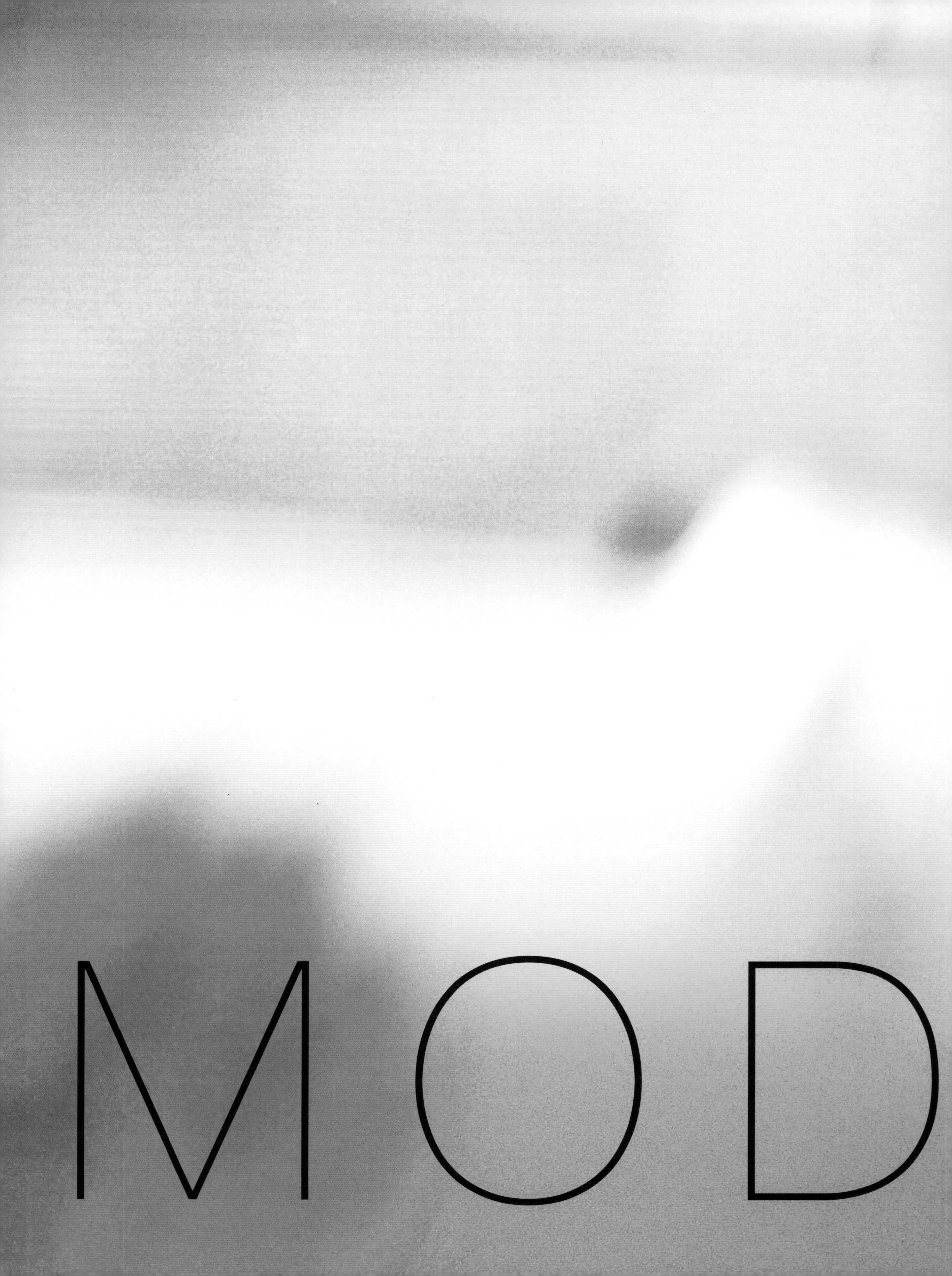
MOD

NEW YORK CITY LOFT

SPACE WITHOUT WALLS

Bold blocks of bright colour can be used to define and divide large open-plan spaces such as this New York City loft. A former warehouse from the 1930s, the building has few frills, but is distinguished by banks of metal-framed windows on two sides, and an attractive roundel high in the eaves. Painted white and flooded with light, a huge empty space such as this needs warmth. Colour is the key to making it home. One important piece of furniture is a good starting point; in this case, it's the sofa, as the majority of the space is given over to the sitting room. In a large space, choose an elegant sofa and cover it in a colour that makes a statement about where the rest of the scheme is going. Black leather sofas in lofts have become something of a cliché, dominating the space and creating a heavy, overtly masculine feel. Here, the choice was orange: an exciting, dynamic contrast with the white, and warm and welcoming without being over-feminine. Further blocks of bright colour bring an immediate vitality throughout the space: alchemilla and shell pink for cushions, curtains and the classic retro chairs that form a loose sociable group around the sofa; more neutral tones enlivened by orange to mark out the dining area; while cooler blues and green predominate in the bedroom upstairs. Linking all of the spaces like a recurring signature is the presence of black and white: in elements of the furniture; in the very few carefully chosen patterns; and in the tassels and trims that give cushions and lampshades their unconventional charm.

BLOCKS OF COLOUR

Choosing some softer, unexpected colours alongside the bright orange gives the scheme subtlety and sophistication. Too many bright or primary colours can be trying on the eye, and the presence of soft pink and alchemilla here is particularly welcome. Pink might not seem the most obvious partner for orange, but works particularly well for the curtains – large panels in plain washed linen that can be pulled right across the windows when needed, forming a coloured backdrop to the space. Central stripes of pink and yellow, bordered with stripes of grey and white, are also used to cover the pair of padded ottomans that double up as low tables and benches.

ABSTRACT INSPIRATION

Housed below the upstairs sleeping platform, the dining area has a much lower ceiling, giving it a more enclosed and intimate feel and helping distinguish it from the neighbouring sitting room. A panel of glass behind the table brings in more light and the illusion of space, as does the pale polished limestone floor and predominantly white and neutral furnishings. Accents of bright orange on the vintage Eiffel chairs (working off the sofa just a few metres away) animate the scene, as do the lights with their whimsical tasselled shades. The curvy amorphous shapes of the furniture, squiggly black leads of the lights, and splashes of bright colour reflected in mirrors and floor call to mind a painting by the abstract-surrealist artist Joan Miro.

COOL AND CALM SLEEPING SPACE

On the upstairs sleeping platform under the eaves pale blues predominate, with accents of turquoise, lime green and a touch of mauve. Black and white also have a strong presence, providing a link to the brighter scheme downstairs and a crucial contrast to the cool, crisp blues and greens. The standard lamp, with its turquoise lining and bobble trim, is as smart as a vintage hat box, but it is the flower print on the floating wall and cushions that steals the show. With all the sensitive detail of an antique etching, it is beautiful without being over-pretty, and has a lightness that prevents it from dominating the room.

CLAS

SICAL

MODERN CLASSIC

UPSCALE ELEGANCE

Grand architecture presents a particular challenge when decorating, and this recently restored Palladian villa is no exception. The sheer size of the rooms – with six metre ceilings on the first floor – and the weight of historical detail can at first seem overwhelming. Thinking boldly is key: rising to the challenge of using pattern to transform these cavernous empty spaces into elegant rooms for contemporary living. The patterns themselves have to be bold. Take the entrance hall, with its sweeping double staircase. Not only is the space itself dramatic; the plasterwork on the ceilings and ironwork on the balustrade are also pretty ornate. A plain colour – even a rich dark one – could easily look austere. But a pattern will have to hold its own alongside the ironwork and the graphic black-and-white floor. The beautiful peony cartouche design selected is perfect. It is large enough to be in scale with the space but has a grace that complements, rather than swamps its surroundings; its colour scheme of black and white on ecru with a touch of deep crimson brings warmth without compromising on clarity. With paintwork picked out in crisp white and furnishings in that same deep pink with black-and-white trims, the result looks and feels effortlessly elegant – a taste of the rooms that follow.

Most of the bedrooms are on the ground floor here, with the main living quarters on the first floor, taking advantage of the stunning views. All of these rooms are enormous, but in each case, a well-chosen pattern – damask flock in the drawing room and a selection of stunning black-and-white prints – give them individuality, character and a certain style.

STRONG CHARACTER

With its incredibly high ceilings, tall doorways and ornamental architraves, the drawing room could seem impersonal, even institutional. Pattern gives it character, and this bold damask flock is just right – a classically inspired design in an unexpected rich turquoise that has been taken up for the other furnishings along with touches of crimson and lime green. Everything has to be strong in a room of this size: patterns, colours, textures, shapes, dimensions. The sofa, for instance, is almost four metres long, and the standard-lamp shades a metre in diameter. Even the details are bold and unfussy: plain silk and velvet for the cushions and plain covers for the large low stools.

BOLD MODERN TONES

Big, bold and beautiful, this combination of intense colour and low modern shapes breathes fresh life into the less formal living room opening off the kitchen. The clear bright colour works well with the plain cotton velvet on the sofa and armchairs: an orangey red almost the colour of a tomato and a strong acid yellow, the red echoing in the interior of the striped lampshade, the paintings, the flowers. Both red and yellow have been used to cover the low square stools that function as ottoman-type tables or can be butted up against one another to make impromptu seating. Together with the striped lamp these chairs look almost like a detail of an abstract painting.

CLEAR COLOUR

At the far end of the living space shown on the previous pages is a state-of-the-art kitchen, concealed behind a white counter top and a bank of white cupboards that keep the clutter out of view. A beautiful black-and-white print has been used for the curtains, and in the dining area is a classic Saarinen white table and chairs in clear, bright colours. The juxtaposition of these clean modern shapes with the curlicue scrolls of the fabric is arresting. Colour is what brings the two contrasting ends of the room together – the same saturated reds and yellows, a chartreuse green, an orange, a pale blue – here looking even more intense against a pure black-and-white backdrop.

VIVID STATEMENT

In a second sitting room, a bold black-and-white print – more black than white this time – forms a distinctive backdrop for restrained amounts of vivid, glowing colour. Crimson, moss and lilac are all present in both the rich embroidered silk stripe used for curtains and the graphic striped velvet on the low modern sofa. The striped black-and-white lamps on their graceful arching supports add a lively touch, with the stripes repeated asymmetrically at some of the windows. The principal colours are repeated in the details: cushions, covers, the backs of the fabulous armchairs: there are no extra accent colours here. Placed around the room, curvaceous classic Platner chairs and low round tables bring softness to a masculine tailored scheme.

MONOCHROME

The downstairs bedrooms have no views and when this is the case it is best to make the atmosphere in the room intimate and inward looking. Shades of grey and white create a restful yet luxurious atmosphere, with a large horizontal stripe behind the four-poster bed and the same stripe, but on silk, with some panels patterned or embroidered, as a bedcover. The ornate wrought-ironwork on the table brings out the fine scrolling patterns on the bedcovers and provides echoes of the grand staircase balustrade.

EASY ELEGANCE

The same mood of restful luxury pervades the bathroom, where classic black-and-white-veined marble lines the walls, and a traditional roll-top bath (its exterior painted grey) holds sway among the other sleek modern fittings: a low key mix of styles that sums up the bold easy elegance that the house is about.

GRA

PHIC

BRIGHT LIGHTS, BIG CITY

CONTEMPORARY RETRO

With its high ceilings and banks of tall narrow windows, this London warehouse bears traces of its semi-industrial past. The challenge was to make it a fun and functional first home for a young artistic couple. Before choosing colours and patterns, the first and most important task was to define the space. The idea of open-plan living appeals to many, but the reality is that everything is on show. Here, the huge expanse of space allowed the opportunity to create a 'floating wall' that would divide the main living area from a study with storage cupboards behind. This clever device leaves the rest of the space clutter-free and ready for an injection of graphic modern pattern. What's new is the mixture: of different scales and different types of pattern, often within very close parameters. And what makes it work is a backdrop of pure unadulterated white, with plenty of plain black and white in the furnishings. Pattern needs room to breathe.

So, in the living room area, an exciting and creative tension is immediately set up between the powerful large-scale black-and-white flower prints used to paper the floating wall and as blinds at the windows, and the smaller, denser, more highly coloured patterns used to cover the low stools, lamps, cushions and other accessories. Acting as a backdrop to the smaller patterns, the big prints serve to highlight their complex beauty and bring out the small amounts of luminous colour: turquoise, lime green and a tiny touch of pink. Keeping the peace in amongst it all are substantial blocks of plain black and white in the form of the white leather sofa (with black seat cushion), white lacquer chair, a Noguchi glass table and dark rug. Playful yet sophisticated, this sets the tone for the innovative and creative use of intense and contrasting colour in the spaces that follow.

FLOATING WALL

Rather than a solid floor-to-ceiling structure that would feel like another room, this floating wall is more like a giant screen. Stopping short of the ceiling and with openings at either end, it hides and divides while still preserving the spaciousness of the apartment. The sitting-room side is papered in a large black-and-white flower print, while the study side is in businesslike black-and-white stripes. As well as a study, this section of the space is home to an entire wall of storage cupboards which are vital for keeping the main body of the place uncluttered. An ingenious and decorative solution, a free-standing wall can also be usefully employed in bedrooms behind the bed.

COOKING AND EATING

At the kitchen end of the open-plan L-shaped space, brighter, warmer colours prevail with one wall painted bubblegum pink and a bold, bright leaf print at the windows. The aim was to keep the functional aspects of the kitchen as low-key as possible, so all is hidden behind a beautiful wooden counter that reads as a regular piece of furniture. Instead, the eye is drawn upwards, to the graphic black-and-white painting on the wall behind, and the vintage light fitting suspended from the ceiling. Again, colour and pattern abound in the details, and the pink, red and orange colour scheme conjures up the vibrant interiors of Mexico.

YOUNG ECLECTIC MIX

The bedroom is an exercise in using contrasting patterns to great effect. The design on the wall behind the bed that acts as backdrop is relatively small – a tight geometric motif that works well as a foil to the larger prints and patterns used for the covers and cushions, and the bold wave print at the windows. It's a young eclectic mix of patterns and florals – what holds them all together is the vibrant pink that runs throughout. Again, the colour scheme of shades of pink, reds, yellows and orange makes more than a nod to Mexico, as does the bold layering of different florals.

DIRECTORY OF RESOURCES

The houses and apartments featured in this book have been decorated using fabrics, wallpapers, paint, furniture, trimmings and accessories from Designers Guild. The main collection names and pieces of furniture, highlighted in **bold**, have been listed below, story by story. Each of these collections and the full range of furniture and accessories may be viewed on the Designers Guild website. For further information, please visit **www.designersguild.com**

MODERN COUNTRY pages 10 – 31
Whitewell printed silks and linens. **Whitewell** wallpapers. **Maitland** weaves, jacquards, velvets and tweeds. **Adelphi** embroidered silks. **Square** sofa in Racine velvet. **Hayward** sofa in Tarleton striped velvet and Racine velvet.

COASTAL RETREAT pages 34 – 51
Brera Alta soft stone-washed pure linen in a wide range of colours. **Brera lino** heavyweight plain linen weave with soft washed texture. **Tiana** Outdoor fabrics.

PARISIAN PIED-A-TERRE pages 54 – 63
Florimund silks, printed fabrics, soft cottons and wallpapers. **Roquelaire** jacquard weaves, embroideries and striped sheers. **Racine** cut velvets and weaves. **Tsuga** linen. **Joseph** sofa in Regence velvet stripe.

ENGLISH MANOR HOUSE pages 66 – 101
Ariana embroidered silks. **Nabucco** weaves. **Baratti** striped silk weave. **Leopold** hexagonal pattern wallpaper. **Bergamasque** flock wallpaper. **Brera** luxurious plain linen/cotton blend. **Varese** velvet. **Nabucco** rugs. **Tailandier** flock wallpaper.

CITY PENTHOUSE pages 104 – 113
Maitland weaves, jacquards, velvets and contemporary tweeds. **Whitewell** flock, print and grasscloth wallpapers. **Square** sofa in Maitland. **Nabucco** rug. **Orsetti** trimmings.

FRENCH CHATEAU pages 116 – 127
Arabella silk, linen and cotton. **Arabella** flock, print and plain wallpapers. **Roumier** weaves. **Darly** wallcoverings. **Ariana** embroidered silks. **Varese** cotton plain velvet. **Chambord** silks, silk dupions and taffetas. **Festival** sofa in Racine. **Balance** daybed in Santuzza. **Hayward** sofa in Varese.

TOWN HOUSE pages 130 – 139
Florimund silks, printed fabrics, soft cottons and wallpapers. Roquelaire jacquard weaves, embroideries and striped sheers. Brera luxurious plain linen/cotton blend.

RETRO MODERN pages 142 – 161
Quarenghi retro jacquard velvet. Roumier soft wools. Brera Alta fabrics, soft stone-washed pure linen in a wide range of colours. Trevelyan woven silks.

REGENCY COUNTRY pages 164 – 185
Pavilion printed silks, linens, cottons and wallcoverings. Nantucket weaves. Cassan weaves. Tiana outdoor fabrics. Domino sofas in Montefiore. Brooklyn sofa in Bridgeport. Gibson chairs in Brera Lino. Gibson daybeds in Montefiore.

LAKESIDE PAVILION pages 188 – 197
Carlu textured wallcoverings. Roumier weaves, soft wools, velvets. Darly wallcoverings. Valadier embroidered striped silks. Balance stools in Leopold. Domino sofas in Deighton and Leblond. Nabucco rugs.

MODERN MANOIR pages 200 – 209
Arabella silk, linen and cotton. Arabella wallcoverings. Darly silks, linens, cottons and wallcoverings. Roumier wools and velvets. Valadier silks. Domino sofas in Deighton and Barbier. Hayward sofas in Willament. Festival sofa and stool in Willament. Festival chair in Vandevelde. Darly rug.

NEW YORK CITY LOFT pages 212 – 221
Brera Alta soft stone-washed pure linen. Brera Lino heavyweight plain linen weave Cassan jacquard, soft velvets and textured weaves. Soho sofa in Brera Lino. Camana ecru rug. Barcelona printed fabrics.

MODERN CLASSIC pages 224 – 237
Arabella silk, linen and cotton. Arabella flock, print and plain wallpapers. Varese cotton plain velvet. Ariana woven embroidered silks with patterns and stripes. Furniture: Joseph daybed in Nabucco. Hayward sofa and chair in Varese.

BRIGHT LIGHTS BIG CITY pages 240 – 249
Manhattan graphics prints. Barcelona printed cottons. Brera Alta soft stone-washed pure linen. Nabucco wallcoverings. Balance sofa in Varese. Balance stools in Manhattan. Domino stool in Brera fabrics.

DESIGNERS GUILD STOCKISTS

Designers Guild Fabrics, Wallcoverings and Home Accessories are available in over 50 countries around the world. For full details on all of our agents and distributors worldwide as well as local stockists in your area, please visit our website www.designersguild.com

DESIGNERS GUILD SHOWROOMS AND HOMESTORES: 267 & 277 Kings Road London SW3 tel 020 7351 5775
76 Marylebone High Street London W1U 5JU tel 020 3301 5826 Designers Guild at Selfridges Oxford Street W1A 1AB tel 020 7629 1234

DESIGNERS GUILD OFFICES
London: 3 Latimer Place W10 6QT **New York**: 28 West 27th Street 2nd Floor New York NY 10001 tel (001212) 967 4540
Paris: 10 rue Saint Nicolas 75012 Paris tel (00331) 44 67 80 70 **Munich**: Ottostrasse 5 80333 München tel (004989) 5434 86161

BRISTOL

SOFA MAGIC
119-121 Coldharbour Road
Redland
Bristol BS6 7SN
01179 248282
info@sofamagic.co.uk
www.sofamagic.co.uk

BERKSHIRE

ALEXANDER JAMES
INTERIORS
55 High Street
Wargrave RG10 8BU
0118 940 2131
info@aji.co.uk

JACQUELINE INTERIORS
18 Brockenhurst Road
South Ascot SL5 9DL
01344 638867
jacquelineinteriors@live.co.uk

BUCKINGHAMSHIRE

JOHN LEWIS
Holmers Farm Way
Cressex Centre
High Wycombe HP12 4NW
014944 62666

MORGAN GILDER
FURNISHINGS
14 High Street Stony Stratford
Milton Keynes MK11 1AF
01908 568674
info@morgangilder.com
www.morgangilder.co.uk

CAMBRIDGESHIRE

CLEMENT JOSCELYNE LTD
17 Fitzroy Street
Cambridge CB1 1ER
01223 442944
cbintdes@clementjoscelyne.co.uk
www.clementjoscelyne.co.uk

CHESHIRE

AUNTY MABEL'S SEAT
37 King Street
Knutsford WA16 6DQ
07812 134084
rebecca@auntymabelsseat.com

CHESHIRE CURTAINS
& INTERIORS LTD
Stanley Mill
Off Churchill Way
Macclesfield SK11 6AU
01625 434121
mail@cheshirecurtains.co.uk

JOHN LEWIS
Wilmslow Road
Cheadle SK8 3BZ
01614 914914

CORNWALL

CASA FINA INTERIORS
29 River Street
Truro TR1 2SJ
01872 270818
mail@casa-fina.co.uk
www.casa-fina.co.uk

TANYA - CURTAINS
BY DESIGN
Camelot Workshop
Penmayne Rock
Wadebridge PL27 6NQ
01208 863183
info@tanyaleech.co.uk
www.tanyaleech.co.uk

ESSEX

CLEMENT JOSCELYNE LTD
9-11 High Street
Brentwood CM14 4RG
01277 225420
bwintdes@clementjoscelyne.co.uk
www.clementjoscelyne.co.uk

LOTTIE MUTTON
45 King Street
Saffron Walden CB11 1EU
01799 522 252
lottiemutton@aol.com

SIMPLY LIVING LIMITED
89 Crouch Street
Colchester CO3 3AT
01206 367333
info@simply-living.co.uk
www.simply-living.co.uk

SOFA DESIGN

301-303 High Road
Loughton IG10 1AH
020 8418 9400
1-4 Uppark Drive
Horns Road
Ilford IG2 6PD
080 8518 0804
www.sofadesign.co.uk

GLOUCESTERSHIRE

FORUM DESIGN
20 West Way
Cirencester GL7 1JA
01285 642282
sales@foruminteriors.co.uk
www.foruminteriors.co.uk

KINGDOM INTERIORS
The Long Barn
Mitre Farm Business Park
Corse Lawn GL19 4NG
01684 291037
info@kingdominteriors.co.uk

UPSTAIRS DOWNSTAIRS
19 Rotunda Terrace
Montpellier Street
Cheltenham GL59 1SW
01242 514023
homeclimatesltd@btinternet.com

HAMPSHIRE

DESIGN HOUSE
7 Great Minster Street
Winchester SO23 9HA
01962 840949
designhousewinchester@
btinternet.com
www.designhousewinchester.co.uk

THE INTERIOR TRADING CO
55-57 Marmion Road
Southsea PO5 2AT
023 9283 8038
enquiries@interior-trading.co.uk

HERTFORDSHIRE

DAVID LISTER INTERIORS
6 Leyton Road
Harpenden AL5 2TL
01582 764270

KENT

BREWERS
Albany House
London Road
Bromley BR1 1DL
020 8460 8551

84 High Street
Sevenoaks TN13 1LP
01732 457613

FABRICS IN CANTERBURY
72 Wincheap
Canterbury CT1 3RS
01227 457555
fabricsincant@aol.com

JOHN LEWIS
Bluewater
Greenhithe DA9 9SA
01322 624123

LEICESTERSHIRE

BARKERS INTERIORS
94 Main Street
Woodhouse Eaves
Loughborough
LE12 8RZ
01509 890473
barkerid@aol.com

ELIZABETH STANHOPE
INTERIORS LTD
27 Mill Street
Oakham Rutland
LE15 6EA
01572 722345

HARLEQUIN INTERIORS
11 Loseby Lane
Leicester LE1 5DR
0116 262 0994
harlequinint@aol.com

INDIGO ACRE
4 Castle Gate House
Bath Street
Ashley de la Zouch LE65 2FH
01530 411744
yvonne@indigoacre.co.uk

LINCOLNSHIRE

UNION INTERIORS
Union Street
Grantham NG31 6NZ
01476 593388
enquires@uniongrantham.com
www.uniongrantham.com

LONDON

BREWERS
283/285 New North Road
N1 7AA
020 7226 2569

327 Putney Bridge Road
SW15 2PG
020 8780 1277

CHARLES PAGE INTERIORS LTD
61 Fairfax Road
NW6 4EE
020 7328 9851
info@charlespage.co.uk

DESIGNERS GUILD
267 & 277 Kings Road
SW3 5EN
020 7351 5775
showroom@designersguild.com

76 Marylebone High Street
London W1U 5JU
020 3301 5826
marylebone@designersguild.com

HARRODS
87-135 Brompton Road
Knightsbridge SW1X 7XL
020 7730 1234

HEAL'S
196 Tottenham Court Road
W1P 9LD
020 7636 1666

INTERIORS OF CHISWICK
454 Chiswick High Road
W4 5TT
020 8994 0073
enquiries@interiorsofchiswick.co.uk

JOHN LEWIS
Oxford Street
W1A 1EX
020 7629 7711

LIBERTY
Regent Street
W1 6AH
020 7734 1234
interiorstyling@liberty.co.uk
www.liberty.co.uk

PETER JONES
Sloane Square
SW1W 8EL
020 7730 3434

REVAMP INTERIORS
26 Knights Hill
West Norwood SE27 0HY
020 8670 5151
revampint@aol.com
www.revampinteriors.com

SALLY BOURNE INTERIORS
26 Muswell Hill Broadway
N10 3RT
0208 444 3031
info2@sallybourneinteriors.co.uk
www.sallybourneinteriors.co.uk

SELFRIDGES
Oxford Street
W1A 1AB
020 7629 1234

MERSEYSIDE

ELAINE CUNNINGHAM
INTERIORS
392 Aigburth Road Aigburth
Liverpool L19 3QD
0845 500 5060
enquires@elainecunningham
interiors.co.uk

NORFOLK

CLEMENT JOSCELYNE LTD
5 Bedford Street
Norwich NR2 1AL
01603 623220
info@clementjoscelyne.co.uk
www.clementjoscelyne.co.uk

NOTTINGHAMSHIRE

JAMIE HEMPSALL LTD
North Beck Low Street East
Drayton DN22 0LN
01777 248463
studio@jamiehempsall.com
www.jamiehempsall.com

NASH INTERIORS
17-19 Carlton Street
NG1 1NL
0115 9507548

OXFORDSHIRE

FAIRFAX INTERIORS
The Old Bakery
High Street Lower Brailes
Nr Banbury OX15 5HW
01608 685301
info@fairfaxinteriors.com

STELLA MANNERING LTD
2 Woodstock Road
Oxford OX2 6HT
01865 557196
stella@stellamanneringltd.co.uk

SOMERSET

PAUL CARTER
Studio Elm House Chip Lane
Taunton TA1 1BZ
01823 330404
thestudio@paulcarter.co.uk
www.paulcarter.co.uk

THE CURTAIN POLE
64 High Street
Glastonbury BA6 9DY
01458 834166
curpole@yahoo.co.uk

SUFFOLK

CLEMENT JOSCELYNE LTD
16 Langton Place
Bury St Edmunds IP33 1NE
01284 753824
buryintdes@clementjoscelyne.co.uk
www.clementjoscelyne.co.uk

EDWARDS OF HADLEIGH
53 High Street
Hadleigh IP7 5AB
01473 827271
info@edwardsonline.co.uk

SITTING PRETTY
16 Friars Street
Sudbury CO10 7GY
01787 880908
sales@sittingprettyinteriors.co.uk
www.sittingprettyinteriors.co.uk

SURREY

BABAYAN PEARCE
INTERIORS
Braeside House High Street
Oxshott KT22 0JP
01372 842437

BREWERS
23-25 High Street
Haslemere GU27 2HG
01428 651717

Albany House
Woodbridge Meadows
Guilford GU1 1BA
01483 568234

CREATIVE INTERIORS
20 Chipstead Station Parade
Chipstead CR5 3TE
01737 555443

GORGEOUS
19 Bell Street Reigate
Surrey RH2 7AD
01737 222846

HEAL'S
Tunsgate
Guildford GU1 3QU
01483 576715

49-51 Eden Street
Kingston upon Thames
KT1 1BW
020 8614 5900

JOHN LEWIS
Wood Street
Kingston upon Thames KT1 1TE
020 8547 3000

PEPPERSTITCH DESIGNS LTD
198 High Street Egham
Surrey TW20 9ED
01784 430501
pepperstitch1@aol.com

SABLE INTERIORS
124 Summer Road
Thames Ditton KT7 0QR
020 8398 9777

SAGE
High Street
Ripley GU23 6BB
01483 224396
reception@sagelifestyle.co.uk

SUSSEX

BREWERS
3 Redkiln Way Horsham
West Sussex RH13 5QH
01403 252345

CORNFIELD HOUSE
32-34 Cornfield Rd
Eastbourne
East Sussex BN21 4QH
01323 727193

SUTTONS FURNISHINGS
Holm Oaks Brighton Road
Clayton Hassocks
West Sussex BN6 9PD
01273 846751
sales@suttonsfurnishings.com

WEST MIDLANDS

JOHN CHARLES INTERIORS
349 Hagley Road Edgbaston
Birmingham B17 8DN
0121 420 3977

JOHN LEWIS
Touchwood
Solihull B91 3RA
0121 704 1121

YORKSHIRE

HOMEWORKS
Charles House
4 Castlegate Tickhill
Doncaster DN11 9QU
01302 743978
interiors@homeworks-tickhill.co.uk

JAMES BRINDLEY
29-31 James Street
Harrogate HG1 1QY
01423 560757
info@jamesbrindley.com

16 High Street
Wetherby LS22 6LT
01937 581451
info@jamesbrindley.com
www.jamesbrindley.com

ROSE & CO INTERIORS
14 Bull Green
Halifax HX1 5AB
01422 381343

2 Millfield House
Huddersfield Road
Thongsbridge
Holmfirth HD9 3JL
01484 688485
enquiries@roseandcointeriors.com
www.roseandcointeriors.com

NORTHERN IRELAND

BEAUFORT INTERIORS LTD
597-599 Lisburn Road
Belfast BT9 7GS

102-106 Main Street
Moira BT67 0LH
02892 2619508
info@beaufortinteriors.co.uk

BEDECK LIMITED
465 Lisburn Road
Belfast BT9 7EZ
028 9066 9828
belfast@bedeckretail.com

The Linen Green
Moygashel Dungannon
BT71 7HB
028 8772 9153
linengreen@bedeckretail.com

FULTONS FINE FURNISHINGS
Hawthorne House
Boucher Crescent
Belfast BT12 6HU
0870 600 0186

55-63 Queen Street
Lurgan BT66 8BN
028 38346765

MOCHA DESIGN
21-23 Spencer Road
Londonderry
Co. Londonderry BT47 6AA
028 7131 1900
sales@mochainteriors.com

TURKINGTONS
Sweep Road Cookstown
Co. Tyrone BT80 8JW
028 86763438

SCOTLAND

CATHERINE HENDERSON
25 Glencairn Drive
Glasgow G41 4QP
0141 423 4321
catherine@catherinehenderson.com

CHELSEA MCLAINE
INTERIOR DESIGN
161 Milngavie Road
Bearsden Glasgow G61 3DY
0141 942 2833
margot@chelseamclaine.
freeserve.co.uk

DESIGNWORKS
38 Gibson Street
Glasgow G12 8NX
0141 339 9520
info@designworks-scotland.co.uk

JEFFREYS INTERIORS
8 North West Circus Place
Edinburgh EH3 6ST
0845 8822 655
jeff@jeffreys-interiors.co.uk

JOHN LEWIS
St James Centre
Edinburgh EH1 3SP
0131 556 9121

Buchanan Galleries
Glasgow G1 2GF
0141 353 6677

WALES

TAYLORS ETC DESIGN
143 Colchester Avenue
Cardiff
S. Glamorgan CF23 7UZ
029 20 358400
www.taylorsetc.co.um

IRELAND

BRIAN S. NOLAN LTD
102 Upper Georges Street
Dun Laoghaire
Co. Dublin 01 2800564
info@briansnolan.ie

O'MAHONY INTERIORS
Enniskeane West Cork
023 47123
omahonyinteriors@eircom.net

ORMOND INTERIOR DESIGN
Castle Court Castle Road
Oranmore
County Galway Ireland
091792210
design@ormondsoftfurnishings.com

SILVER RIVER INTERIORS
Offaly Street, Tullamore,
County Offaly
057 9329689
info@silverriver.ie

AUSTRALIA

RADFORD FURNISHINGS
HEAD OFFICE AND
SHOWROOM
Level 1
146 Burwood Road
Hawthorn
VIC 3122
tel +61 3 9818 7799
fax +61 3 9818 5531
sales@radfordaus.com
www.radfordfurnishings.com

NEW ZEALAND

ICON TEXTILES LTD
HEAD OFFICE AND
SHOWROOM
Level 2
262 Thorndon Quay
Wellington 6011
tel 00 64 4 4741076
sales@icontextiles.co.nz
www.icontextiles.co.nz

ACKNOWLEDGMENTS

ELSPETH THOMPSON   1961 – 2010
Elspeth has always been an inspiration to work with. Over a period of fifteen years working on eight books together, she transformed visual ideas into sensitive prose with understanding and brilliance. A joy to be with – her spiritual aura and intelligence are irreplaceable. We celebrate her thoughtful and intuitive words within these pages.

My thanks to our uniquely special team – Anne, Meryl, James, Jo, Liza and of course, Elspeth who will be greatly missed by us all.

To my exceptionally talented team at Designers Guild: so many who have been involved in different ways, I really appreciate their contribution.

Special thanks to Alison and Simon Jeffreys, Mark Homewood and Michael Sharp, Liza and Matt Giles, Greg Wooten, Holger Nicolai, Tim Jasper, Thomas Unterdorfer, Becker Interieur und Design in Ibiza.

First published in 2010 by Quadrille Publishing Limited
Alhambra House, 27–31 Charing Cross Road, London WC2H 0LS

Editorial director Anne Furniss
Designer Meryl Lloyd
Tricia Guild's creative manager Jo Willer
Creative stylist Liza Giles
Copy editor Sarah Mitchell
Editorial assistant Louise McKeever
Production Marina Asenjo, Vincent Smith

© Text Elspeth Thompson 2010 © Photographs James Merrell 2010
© Design and layout Quadrille Publishing Ltd 2010

British Library Cataloguing in Publication Data
A catalogue record for this book is available from the British Library

ISBN 978 1 84400 845 2

Printed and bound in China
10 9 8 7 6 5 4 3 2 1